THE WAR
WITHIN

THE WAR

W I T H I N

Gaining Victory in the Battle
for Sexual Purity

Robert Daniels

CROSSWAY BOOKS • WHEATON, ILLINOIS
A DIVISION OF GOOD NEWS PUBLISHERS

The War Within

Published by Crossway Books
        a division of Good News Publishers
        1300 Crescent Street
        Wheaton, Illinois 60187

Editing: Ted Griffin

Cover design: Cindy Kiple

Cover photograph: Jim Whitmer

First printing, 1997

Printed in the United States of America

Library of Congress Cataloging-in-Publication Data
Daniels, Robert, 1952-
   The war within : gaining victory in the battle for sexual
purity / Robert Daniels.
     p.   cm.
   ISBN 0-89107-933-5
   1. Sex—Religious aspects—Christianity. 2. Men—Religious life.
   3. Sexual ethics   I. Title.
BT708.D36 1997
241'.66—dc21   96-45359

05		04		03		02		01		00		99		98	
15	14	13	12	11	10	9	8	7	6	5	4	3	2		

This book is dedicated to my wonderful, loving, and understanding wife. Without her love, acceptance, availability, encouragement, and forgiveness I would not have written this book. I love you with all my heart and am so grateful that God brought you into my life.

CONTENTS

Acknowledgments   ix

Preface   xi

1   My Secret Life   *13*

2   "I Didn't Know It Was Fornication"   *27*

3   The Supreme Battle   *39*

4   Dead to Sin—Alive to God   *51*

5   Protected by the Promises of God   *61*

6   His Word in My Heart   *69*

7   Face to Face, Side by Side   *75*

8   On Guard!   *87*

9   Our Defeated But Devious Foe   *97*

10   When Past Hurts Make Us Hide   *109*

11   A Call to Self-Discipline   *123*

12   The Discipline of the Lord   *135*

13   Dealing with Consequences and Casualties   *145*

14   Battle Partners   *175*

15   What About Masturbation?   *183*

16   Drunk or Filled?   *191*

17   Smart Bombs and Cybersex   *197*

18   Down But Not Out   *205*

A Final Word   *215*

Bibliography   *220*

A Prayer   *221*

Appendix   *223*

ACKNOWLEDGMENTS

Many thanks to the men who have loved me and have given their time to read and comment on the rough drafts of this manuscript. Thanks to Dr. Rob Niewoehner, Pete Gerhard, George Janvier, Dave Cook, Dave Welch, Bob Tobey, Dr. Jim Natter, and Dr. Andy Strachan. A special thanks to Mike Wagner, who devoted many hours of time and lots of red ink giving constructive comments and suggestions. Thanks, Mike! Thanks also to Andy Melton for help in getting the manuscript printed. Thanks also to Bobbie Landon of Protect the Child Resource Network of Monterey County for her timely editorial comments.

I would also like to thank the following men for discipling, mentoring, and loving me over the years: Chris Christian, Rusty Stephens, Campbell Kidd, Doug Koenigsberg, Ed Bogner, John Ed Robertson, Jimmie Truhlar, Don Lanier, Paul Drake, Ron Holechek, Wayne Haddock, Bill Greenaway, Gene Smith, Larry Matthews, Mike Slone, Dave Yumen, Tom Love, Dave Cook, and Willie Page, I know there are many others that I have forgotten. Please forgive me. I would not be in a position of believing God for forgiveness without your encouragement and love and examples of faith.

A special thanks to Dr. Jerry White and to Jerry Bridges for their kind endorsements of this book and for their comments that helped strengthen the manuscript. Also, thank you to all the dear people who have prayed for me personally in my own struggles for purity and for this project.

Most of all I want to acknowledge the Lord Jesus Christ and His saving and empowering grace and forgiveness.

PREFACE

I'm not proud of what my life was once like. Though a believer in Christ, I was out of fellowship with God, walking my own way, blinded by the lust of sexual sin. I was daily involved in pornography and masturbation. Even though I strayed, God didn't. Instead, He drew me back to Himself by convicting me of my waywardness through Luke 22:31-32: "Simon, Simon, Satan has asked to sift you as wheat. But I have prayed for you, Simon, that your faith may not fail. And when you have turned back, strengthen your brothers." As I read these verses, I knew that God was speaking both *to* me and *about* me. I reread them: "Bob, Bob, Satan has asked to sift you as wheat. But I have prayed for you, Bob, that your faith may not fail. And when you have turned back, strengthen your brothers." My soul was thrilled that the Lord was personally pleading in prayer for me, as He does for all God's children (see Romans 8:34).

I felt loved by Jesus. I felt known by God and a sense of being owned or being part of His family. I also felt scared, knowing that Satan wanted to attack and defeat me. I saw in this verse my "marching orders"—to repent and to strengthen the faith of my brothers.

I have repented and continue to repent as the Lord faithfully shows me my nakedness, my blindness, and the impoverished state of my soul. This book is an attempt to obey the second command of that verse—to strengthen the faith of my brothers.

Before I started applying the principles that the Lord taught me, I felt hopelessly defeated and constantly waiting for deliverance. But when I started obeying the commands and principles of spiritual warfare, I started experiencing freedom from the guilt and oppression of sexual sin. Psalm 40:1-3 describes the before-and-after feelings of my situation: "I waited patiently for the LORD; he turned to me and heard my cry. He lifted me out of the slimy pit, out of the mud and mire; he set my feet on a rock and gave me a firm place to stand. He put a new song in my mouth, a hymn of praise to our God. Many will see and fear and put their trust in the LORD."

Certainly God desires our sexual purity. But much more than this—within the framework of God's purpose for a husband and wife in marriage, sexual relations become pure and holy, a beautiful picture of our Lord's glorious intimate love for His own (Eph. 5:25-32).

It is my prayer that "many will see and fear and put their trust in the LORD" and will experience the exhilarating energy that comes from sexual purity and the joy of walking in fellowship with the risen Lord Jesus Christ.

My Secret Life

I remember walking through our kitchen one day as a seventh grader. My new stepmother asked me, "What do you want to be when you grow up?" I thought, "This isn't a fair question; she doesn't really know me." I'm sure she didn't expect the answer I blurted out: "A male prostitute." When I saw the look of horror on her face, I smirked and ran on my way.

I had gotten the idea after reading an adult book with the theme of younger men who were hired by rich, older, lonely women to have sex with them. In my way of thinking, this was a great job! I had been reading pornographic books and looking at nude pictures for several years. I had begun to masturbate and was engaging in that practice two or three times a day.

The next day my parents searched my room and removed my private collection of pornography. I was angry and decided to keep quiet about my sexual desires and practices. This self-imposed silence about deep issues would plague me for years. Sadly, I would eventually find out that many other men were hurt by their silence also.

My father and stepmother instilled in us children a desire for higher education. Sometime during the seventh grade my father planted the idea in my head to apply to the Naval Academy in Annapolis, Maryland. I was the fourth of six kids, and I knew my folks didn't have the money to send me to college. So getting into the Naval Academy became the consuming pursuit of my life for the next five years. I read the entrance catalog and found out what the incoming plebe (freshman) class looked like: 90 percent were either valedictorian or salutatorian in high school; 95 percent were involved in some form of student leadership of clubs or student government; 85 percent attended church youth groups or choirs. Most were involved in high school athletics or band.

These activities became my goals. I ran for president of the Spanish Club and got elected. I played basketball, tennis, and baseball, achieving success in each sport. I attended our local Presbyterian church. I wanted my life to exactly mirror the lives of those who made it into the Naval Academy.

Our church was controversial. The Viet Nam War was in progress, and our pastor decided to light a "Peace" candle in our church sanctuary and keep it lit until "the American Imperialistic Army" came home from Viet Nam. My father had earned a Purple Heart in World War II when a Japanese *kamikaze* shot his kneecap off during an attack in the South Pacific. Every Sunday, our pastor would speak out against the war, and every Sunday my dad would come away angry, cussing out the pastor for his views. On TV each night Walter Cronkite would tell how many American boys died that day or week in Viet Nam.

There was a lack of peace nationally and locally in our small town in Arkansas. This unrest worked into my own heart. How could I go to a war that was being questioned morally? Could I fight and possibly kill someone? What about my goals of a free college education? What about my trying to go to the Naval Academy? These questions were all constantly swimming around in my head.

My dad would take one position on the morality of the war, my pastor a different one. Whom could I turn to for an answer? My high school guidance counselor was a nice lady, but being close to eighty years old, she seemed a bit out of touch to me. I was not on good speaking terms with my dad, and I felt that my pastor was irrelevant and unapproachable.

My high school basketball coach invited our whole team to attend a concert in Fayetteville, Arkansas. This concert was put on by college kids who would sing popular songs of the day, followed by personal stories of how they had met Jesus. I'd never heard a testimony before, so I was intrigued to hear people talk about Jesus as if He were real and alive.

I had always wondered how someone who had died 2,000 years ago could have any effect on me. I knew all the terms of religion—heaven, hell, resurrection, judgment, etc. But I didn't know how it all fit together. I had often wondered about these things as I sat in church Sunday after Sunday.

One of the singers shared a quotation from the Bible, Jeremiah 29:11, 13, that really pierced my heart: "'I know the thoughts I have for you,' declares the LORD, 'plans to prosper you and not to harm you, plans to give you hope and a future . . . You will seek me and find me when you seek me with all your heart.'" I wanted to know what God's plans were for me. Did those plans include the Naval Academy? Could I—should I—go to war?

At the end of the concert, an invitation was given. In one way I wanted to go forward, but I didn't want to make a fool of myself.

I was, after all, the captain of the team. What would the others think? I moved one of my feet about six inches toward the aisle. I happened to be standing next to our coach, a big man about 6' 3". He must have realized that the Spirit was working in me because when I took that baby step, he grabbed me by the arm and yanked me out into the aisle.

When I got to the front of the church, a man asked me if I was there to "rededicate myself to the Lord." I said, "I've never dedicated my life to Him, so how could I rededicate it?" That comment qualified me go into a different line, where one of the singers shared a tract with me called *Four Spiritual Laws*.

I had heard about Jesus, and I knew I was a sinner. But that tract clearly showed that Jesus died *for me*. For the first time in my life I understood the significance of Jesus' death on the cross. That night I asked the Lord Jesus Christ to come into my life to be my Lord and Savior. What a glorious feeling it was to be set free from sin—to know that I would spend eternity in heaven.

That feeling, however, was short-lived. As I was doing pull-ups on a tree in our front yard several weeks later, I was thinking about how wonderful it was that I was going to heaven when I suddenly thought, "Surely, it can't be that easy! You have to earn something as valuable as that." Just like that, I lost the joy and peace I'd had. I was confused about Jesus and what He had done and how I was connected to Him. I was confused about my salvation, though I kept praying in the hope there was a God listening.

Each night I would pray, "Lord, let me into the Naval Academy. I don't know Your perfect will, but please let me in." And God granted my request. And I knew it was God who had gotten me into that place. In the physical exams prior to entrance, one of the doctors had found a heart murmur. I also had hay fever, and my eyes were not 20/20. Also, a month before I was supposed to enter, I got into a fight and broke my jaw. I had no ties with politicians. (The closest I came to being political was a summer job in the county courthouse as a janitor.) Despite all this, I made it into the Academy. This was clearly God's doing.

All the questions I had about being in the military, killing, and the morality of war were erased when I received my appointment. I knew in my heart that God had opened the door. I would have been disqualified physically from entrance if the Lord had not intervened. Because the door could so easily have been closed but wasn't, I concluded that it was God's plan for me to go into the military.

As it turned out, if I had not entered the Naval Academy at that time, I would have had to go into the military a year later. The draft was still in place, and my draft number for the year I was eligible was number 1!

Within the first week after I arrived at the Naval Academy, my roommate told me about his sexual exploits with different women. He asked me about my sexual history. "I'm a virgin," I said. "Well, we can fix that," he told me. He also found out I'd never been drunk. When word spread to my classmates, several promised me they would personally supervise my entrance rites into the world of "real manhood" during our summer cruise immediately following plebe year.

Our cruise would take us for a week-long visit to Auckland, New Zealand, then on to Sydney, Australia, and then homeward bound to Long Beach, California, via Pearl Harbor, Hawaii. On the way to New Zealand, every time I saw these fellows, they would smile and tell me how great it would be when we got into port. The only problem was, I suffered a total lack of peace. I felt sex should be reserved for marriage; my Presbyterian background of morality was peeking through. At the same time, I wanted the other guys' approval. I didn't know how to escape my dilemma.

At that time I met another midshipman, A.J. Christian. Chris had written previously to some missionaries who were serving with the Navigators at the University of Auckland. I had never heard of the Navigators before. Chris invited me to go with him to the missionary's home and to attend a "rally." I didn't know what a rally was, but I knew it wasn't a bar and a prostitute, so I went.

Chris didn't know if I was a believer or not. Later that day the missionary, David Bradford, asked me if I was a follower of Jesus. After figuring out I was a baby believer who had no spiritual roots, Chris started teaching me about the Christian life. He spent hours teaching me how to pray, the importance of Bible reading and Bible study, etc.

That night for the first time in my life I heard a man proclaim the Word of God with authority. John Crawford, another Navigator missionary, seemed to be able to quote the entire Bible from memory. He talked about the virtues of disciplined Scripture memorization. As John looked out over the audience of sixty New Zealand college kids and a few American sailors (I was sitting in the front row), he said, "Many people talk about Scripture memory, but not many people . . ." His voice was rising now. He looked me right in the eyes and yelled, "DO IT." My heart jumped, my body jumped, my spirit jumped. I thought, "I'll DO IT, I'll DO IT. I'll memorize Scripture. Just don't yell at me again." Right after the meeting I borrowed five dollars from a friend and purchased the Navigators Topical Memory System (TMS).

The next day while sitting in a hot tub, David Bradford, Chris, and several others started reviewing verses they had memorized.

It seemed as if all the fellows who were with me had ten to fifteen verses memorized. I didn't have any memorized yet, so they asked me to go to the other end of the pool and learn a few verses before rejoining them.

I really wanted to be accepted by these fellows. I saw that Chris and Rusty, one of the other midshipmen there, showed brotherly love for each other. I didn't have anyone who enjoyed my company like that, who loved me like that. However, when I was sent to the other end of the pool, I felt rejected by the very folks I wanted to love me. I so longed to be accepted and cared for, I reasoned that if memorizing Scripture was the way to be accepted by this group, that is what I would do. The TMS included sixty verses, so I made it my goal to beat Chris and Rusty through those verses.

I accomplished that goal but didn't stop with the sixty verses. Within several years, I memorized over 1,000 verses and had grown much in my knowledge of God and His Word. However, head knowledge is not the same as heart knowledge. I still had not figured out how to apply God's Word to the self-destructive areas of my life. I mistakenly thought that if only I could memorize enough verses, God would love me, my Christian brothers would accept me, and my struggles with pornography and masturbation would be resolved. Not so.

Every bathroom at the Naval Academy had pornography in the stalls. The bulletin boards were covered with centerfolds from *Playboy* and *Penthouse* magazines. I continued the practice of looking for and lusting at pornography. All the verses I had memorized about the Lord just made me feel more guilty. No one else mentioned that they struggled with this issue. No one talked about it. I felt I was the only one. I doubted the truth of 1

Corinthians 10:13, "No temptation has seized you except what is common to man. And God is faithful; he will not let you be tempted beyond what you can bear. But when you are tempted, he will also provide a way out so that you can stand up under it." Since no Christian brother I knew was talking about his sexual sins, I wrongly assumed I was the only one and thus my temptation was not "common to man." I didn't believe the second part of this verse either. I could find no way of escape until years later.

One of the first messages I heard as a Christian presented the idea of being a finisher. Lots of believers start the race well, but not all endure in their walk with God, the speaker stated. I wanted to be one of those who finish the race well. Psalm 27:4 says, "One thing I ask of the LORD, this is what I seek: that I may dwell in the house of the LORD all the days of my life." This became one of the guiding verses of my life. It is also a prayer that I have prayed more than any other. "Lord, please don't let me stumble or fall or be disqualified from the race or be a quitter. Please let me finish well." For over a year when I first started growing as a Christian, I prayed this almost every day. I believe now that God was answering this cry of my heart when I began to doubt, though I didn't see it at the time.

I figured that if 1 Corinthians 10:13 wasn't true, maybe other verses weren't true either. And if some other verses weren't true, maybe the Bible wasn't true. And if the Bible wasn't true, maybe God wasn't really God. I'll talk more about this later.

As I mentioned earlier, the Lord liberated me from my downward spiral through Luke 22:31-32, "Simon, Simon, Satan has asked to sift you as wheat. But I have prayed for you, Simon, that your faith may not fail. And when you have turned back, strengthen your brothers." These verses were rescue verses in my life. What an encouragement it was to know that my Savior was working on my behalf to protect me from the Enemy's assaults. About the same time two verses in the Psalms spoke to me: "The LORD delights in the way of the man whose steps he has made firm; though he stumble, he will not fall, for the LORD upholds him with his hand" (37:23-24). Together these two passages revealed to me what was going on spiritually during that year and a half of intense struggle: Satan had desired to have me; I had fallen, and my faith had almost failed; the Lord Jesus had prayed for me, and He kept me from falling headlong. Now I needed to repent, turn back to Him, and strengthen the faith of my brothers.

After graduation from the Naval Academy and a year's training in nuclear power, my first ship was the USS *Enterprise*, stationed in Alameda, California, near San Francisco. At that time warship personnel were all male; no women were allowed. Pornography was readily available. Almost every bathroom had a stash of indecent literature. It was easy to look, lust, and act out the lust. I continued to engage in my sinful habits. I was living a double life. My private life was consumed with lust and guilt. My more public life was spent in the pursuit of God and in efforts to help men find Him. I felt trapped and didn't know how to rid myself of these sexual desires.

I found the Lord to be faithful through all this, though I was not. In Thailand we pulled into a port, and I took several young disciples of the Lord with me on a shopping trip. After spending the day shopping and exploring the city of Bangkok, we went into a large, reputable, American-owned hotel where we thought we could get a legitimate massage, on which I spent my last twenty dollars. Much to my surprise, the masseuse's whole purpose was to turn me on sexually, which she did. Blinded by lust, I asked her about sex. She quoted a price of twenty dollars. I had just spent all my money on shopping and on the massage. In this way God delivered me.

I was so close to fornication, and possibly close to receiving a sexually transmitted disease (STD). (Thailand is one of the leading countries in the world for the distribution of the HIV virus.) I had been ready to throw away all my efforts of keeping pure for the sake of a few moments of illicit pleasure, simply because I let myself get too close to sin. Proverbs 5:8 says, "Do not go near the door of [an adulteress's] house, keep to a path far from her." I broke the counsel of that verse. I had the desire and the opportunity to sin, but, thank God, I didn't have the money.

Another time in my Navy career, I was stationed on a little island in the middle of the San Francisco Bay Area called Treasure Island. The Navy has a small training base there, and I was assigned to a six-week-long course prior to reporting to my next command. I lived in the BOQ (Bachelor Officer's Quarters). The physical arrangements of the rooms were a suite format (a common bathroom separating two living/bedroom areas). One Sunday morning, after showering, shaving, and dressing, I had a devotional time with a fellow Christian naval officer named Dale. We had a wonderful time of prayer and reading the Bible together. After we finished our devotions, Dale left to return to his ship; we were going to have brunch together upon his return. I went and purchased a newspaper, returned to my room, and started reading it. I was fully dressed and sitting on my bed. While reading, I felt a strange presence, as if someone were looking at me.

I looked over at the bathroom door and saw it was opened a

crack. Through the crack I could see someone looking at me. When our eyes met, a beautiful girl walked right into my room! I couldn't believe it. I jumped up, and she threw herself onto the bed. I was embarrassed to have a woman lying on my bed, afraid someone would see her and assume . . . I also knew Dale was going to return soon. What would my Christian brother think?

Praise God, I had no desire to approach her sexually. When she realized I was not interested, she left the same way she came. I quickly locked the bathroom door. By day she cleaned rooms at the BOQ, and at night she was a prostitute. She had spent the night with my suite-mate. Again God had protected me. I had the opportunity to sin sexually, but I did not have the desire. Praise God that I had worshiped with a brother that very morning and as a result, at that critical moment of temptation I had no desire to sin.

God delivered me again when I first arrived in San Diego. I had been transferred to another ship. This time I was alone, not knowing many people, in a strange town, full of personal insecurities. Late one night I was full of lust. My plan was to call a massage business. Not one of the "businesses" I called would send someone to the house where I was staying. They all thought I was a vice cop and would bust them. Because I was not a regular customer, no one would come.

At first I was mad. Mad at the "businesses," mad at myself for trying to contact a prostitute, mad at God for giving me an overwhelming sex drive. Later, after spending time with the Lord in confession and prayer, I repented of my efforts to sin. Again God had delivered me, even though I didn't want His protection for a period of time. I had the money to sin and the desire to sin but could not find the opportunity to sin.

As I look back on my life, I am amazed at God's merciful protection of me. He has indeed been my Deliverer. When I had the desire to sin, I either did not have the opportunity or the money to sin. When I had the opportunity, I lacked the desire. When I had the opportunity and the desire, I lacked the money. Praise God for His merciful help in avoiding a fall into open sin. Proverbs 2:16-19 says, "It [wisdom] will save you also from the adulteress, from the wayward wife with her seductive words, who has left the partner of her youth and ignored the covenant she made before God. For her house leads down to death and her paths to the spirits of the dead. None who go down to her return or attain the paths of life." The Hebrew word translated "save . . . from" means "to deliver; to be snatched out of; to free oneself; to tear apart; to escape." God helped me escape from loose women.

When you are feeling a desire to sin, call out to God, our protector. Psalm 50:14-15 says, "Sacrifice thank offerings to God, fulfill your vows to the Most High, and *call upon me in the day of trouble; I will deliver you, and you will honor me*" (emphasis mine).

As I continued growing spiritually over a period of several years, I kept crying out to God for help, healing, deliverance—whatever I needed to stop my habits of masturbation and lusting over pornography. God was slowly and mercifully teaching me lessons about my life and His plans and provisions for purity. When I recognized God's standards for sexual purity, I had been a believer for several years but was masturbating three to four times a day. As the years went by, I learned lessons that helped me to cut that down to once a day, then once a week, then once a month until now, once every few years. It is still a battle for me, but the time increments keep increasing between lapses.

Temptation, instead of being like a 500-pound gorilla sitting on my chest, is now like a five-year-old trying to harass me. The spiritual lessons God has taught me are deep, indispensable truths that, when applied, guarantee success in the struggle for purity. The battle now for me is not learning new lessons, but rather continuing to apply what I know. This is still a battle for me. In my own strength I continue to be vulnerable, weak, and, using Navy terminology, sinkable. If I don't apply the lessons the Lord has taught me, I won't finish well. I won't lose my salvation, but I will lose heavenly reward and will disgrace my Savior in this life.

I know from Scripture that I am destined to be holy, spotless, and blameless before God. He has promised that I will be pure for all eternity. He will give me and all believers a new body, a body not infected by sin, though in this life we still struggle against wickedness. I also know from Scripture that Jesus died for me and has forgiven me of all my sin—past, present, and future.

All my sins are forgiven. I am destined to live in holiness forever. But what about now, en route to the forever? That is what I need help on. How can I "abstain from sinful desires, which wage war against [my] soul," as 1 Peter 2:11 says? How can I win or survive in this battle for purity?

The lessons the Lord has taught me are what I want to pass on to you. As you continue reading, I pray that the Lord will strengthen your faith and that you will find help in your battle for sexual purity.

KEY PRINCIPLE

When we stray from God's will for us, Jesus keeps praying for us and protects us as we cry out to Him.

KEY VERSES

"Simon, Simon, Satan has asked to sift you as wheat. But I have prayed for you, Simon, that your faith may not fail. And when you have turned back, strengthen your brothers" (Luke 22:31-32).

DISCUSSION QUESTIONS

1. What parts of my testimony can you most identify with? Why?

2. When did you first look at pornography? Is it an ongoing problem with you? What effects is this having on your life and on those around you?

3. Examine again 1 Corinthians 10:13. Do you find it difficult to accept this verse as true? Who do you know that honestly shares their secret life with you? Do you have someone you trust with whom you can share your struggles?

"I Didn't Know
It Was Fornication"

My wife and I attend the Navy chapel where we are assigned to minister. It is our habit to try and meet each new sailor that comes through the chapel doors. We want to make them all feel welcome and try to figure out where they stand with the Lord. One day a young naval officer whom I'll call David came into the chapel. David had a clear testimony as to when and how he became a believer. David also said he was engaged to be married and that in a couple of weeks his fiancée was coming to town to visit him. I told David that if his fiancée needed a place to stay while in town, she could stay with us. David's response was, "Thanks for asking, but she will stay with me in my BOQ room," the BOQ being a hotel for unmarried officers found on most military bases. I had been in this particular BOQ and knew the rooms had one single bed.

I didn't say anything to David at that time, but I knew he was probably having sex with his fiancée. All week long I was troubled about the situation. How could this believer in the Lord Jesus be doing this—and openly tell someone he had just met that he was doing it? I prayed about this and decided I should ask him about it. Maybe his relationship with her was platonic, nonsexual.

Later on that week I met David in his BOQ room. I asked him, "Could I ask you a personal question?" David said, "Sure, go ahead." I asked, "When your fiancée comes to visit you, she sleeps with you. Does that mean you have sex with her?" Without batting an eye, even rather proudly, David said, "Sure, we do it all the time!"

I asked him if we could talk about that. He agreed, so I asked him to read aloud Ephesians 5:3 from the *Revised Standard Version* Bible I had with me: "But fornication and all impurity or covetousness must not even be named among you, as is fitting among saints." He read it to me, looked up, and said, "So what? How does this apply to me?" I asked him, "Do you know what the word 'fornication' means?" David said, "No."

David was a college graduate who had been involved in discipleship groups for over three years. I asked him, "Do you have a dictionary?" I had him look up the word *fornication* in *Webster's Dictionary*. He read the definition out loud: "Fornication: sexual intercourse between unmarried people." I then asked him to read Ephesians 5:3 again. As he read, I silently prayed, "Lord, may Your Holy Spirit convict David of sin. Please use Your Word to give him understanding. May it penetrate his heart and soul. I don't know what else to do—You must do a work here."

David read the verse again, then read the definition of fornication again in the dictionary. He did a third time as well. He then looked up and with tears in his eyes said in a broken voice, "Nobody ever told me this was wrong. I have had sex with lots of girls. All my Christian group leaders in college knew I was having sex, but they didn't say anything to me. Why didn't they tell me this wasn't what God wants?"

I couldn't answer his questions. There may have been ignorance of the teachings of Scripture on the part of those leaders. Or their silence may have been due to rebellion, moral failure, or whatever. I don't know why others failed him, but I know that God told me to speak to David about his sin. Colossians 1:28-29 says, "We proclaim him, admonishing and teaching everyone with all wisdom, so that we may present everyone perfect in Christ. To this end I labor, struggling with all his energy, which so powerfully works in me." After David had told me about the sleeping arrangements with his fiancée, I had an obligation to David—first to teach him about holiness, and then, if he already knew about God's standards, to warn him about his sinful actions.

Sadly, David was not an isolated case. According to some sources, adultery within the church is almost statistically the same as adultery outside the church, and young people who attend youth groups are as sexually active as those who do not attend church. Even if these reports are not accurate, it is certainly true that many believers fall into sexual sin, thus mirroring at least to some extent our society.

According to the Center for Communicable Disease, twenty-three sexually transmitted diseases are at epidemic levels in the U.S. AIDS has become a major killer of young adults. Clearly, the battle for sexual purity is widespread, fierce, and deadly. It affects every one of us. James 1:27 says, "Religion that God our Father accepts as pure and faultless is this: to look after orphans and widows in their distress and *to keep oneself from being polluted by the world*" (emphasis mine). One of the battles we as Christian men face is to live our lives in this world, which is saturated with sexual perversion and sin, and yet be unstained and undefiled. To win the battle, we must know what our Master desires and expects of us and then obey what He tells us.

God is the one who has set the standards of what is right and wrong. God is the one who created man and set up for man His rules and guidelines as to what is pure and what is impure. He gave very clear instructions in the Law in the Old Testament and in the epistles in the New Testament as to what kinds of behavior in all areas of life are acceptable and what kinds of behavior are unacceptable. In the area of sexuality, God has very clearly defined what is pure and what is impure. Consider the following samples from one Old Testament book, Leviticus:

"No one is to approach any close relative to have sexual relations. I am the LORD."

—18:6

"Do not take your wife's sister as a rival wife and have sexual relations with her while your wife is living."

—18:18

"Do not have sexual relations with your neighbor's wife and defile yourself with her."

—18:20

"Do not lie with a man as one lies with a woman; that is detestable."

—18:22

"Do not have sexual relations with an animal and defile yourself with it. A woman must not present herself to an animal to have sexual relations with it; that is a perversion."

—18:23

> *"Consecrate yourselves and be holy, because I am the LORD your God. Keep my decrees and follow them. I am the LORD, who makes you holy."*
>
> *—20:7-8*

There are a lot of don'ts listed in Leviticus 18:6—20:8, many more than we have taken the time to list here. God's purpose in this section of His Word was to define what is holy in sexual behavior. Why? "You are to be holy to me because I, the LORD, am holy, and I have set you apart from the nations to be my own" (20:26). A large part of what the Creator thinks is holy is connected with sexual behavior.

The passages in Leviticus form the letter of the law, which many were able to perform in large measure. But Jesus raised the standard even higher—beyond the *letter* to the *spirit* of the Law. "You have heard that it was said, 'Do not commit adultery.' But I tell you that anyone who looks at a woman lustfully has already committed adultery with her in his heart" (Matthew 5:27). That which we think, dream, and fantasize about is just as important to our holy Father as the things we actually do. But this must all conform to His standards, not ours. The words of David in Psalm 19:14 come to mind: "May the words of my mouth and the meditation of my heart be pleasing in your sight, O Lord, my Rock and my Redeemer."

The topic of sexual purity is not limited to Jesus' Sermon on the Mount. Consider the following New Testament passages:

> *Put to death, therefore, whatever belongs to your earthly nature:* sexual immorality, impurity, lust, *evil desires and greed, which is idolatry.*
>
> *—Colossians 3:5 (emphasis mine)*

It is God's will that you should be holy; that you should avoid sexual immorality; that each of you should learn to control his own body in a way that is holy and honorable, not in passionate lust like the heathen, who do not know God; and that in this matter no one would wrong his brother or take advantage of him. The Lord will punish men for all such sins, as we have already told you and warned you. For God did not call us to be impure, but to live a holy life. Therefore, he who rejects this instruction does not reject man but God, who gives you his Holy Spirit.
—*1 Thessalonians 4:3*

Do you not know that the wicked will not inherit the kingdom of God? Do not be deceived: Neither the sexually immoral nor idolaters nor adulterers nor male prostitutes nor homosexual offenders *nor thieves nor the greedy nor drunkards nor slanderers nor swindlers will inherit the kingdom of God.*
—*1 Corinthians 6:9-10 (emphasis mine)*

But the cowardly, the unbelieving, the vile, the murderers, the sexually immoral, *those who practice magic arts, the idolaters and all liars—their place will be in the fiery lake of burning sulfur. This is the second death.*
—*Revelation 21:8 (emphasis mine)*

As you can see, the Scriptures are full of teachings, guidelines, prohibitions, and warnings in this area of sexual conduct. God has given a clear standard for sexual purity. But *no one* could meet or keep the standard. We were all condemned to die and to be separated from God for all eternity; we are all doomed. Romans 3:19-24 says:

Now we know that whatever the law says, it says to those who are under the law, so that every mouth may be silenced and the whole world held accountable to God. Therefore no one will be declared righteous in his sight by observing the law; rather, through the law we become conscious of sin. But now a righteousness from God, apart from law, has been made known, to which the Law and the Prophets testify. This righteousness from God comes through faith in Jesus Christ to all who believe. There is no difference, for all have sinned and fall short of the glory of God, and are justified freely by his grace through the redemption that came by Christ Jesus.

We know that through Jesus Christ and the power of the Holy Spirit we can now fulfill the requirements of the law. Romans 8:2-4 says:

. . . through Christ Jesus the law of the Spirit of life set me free from the law of sin and death. For what the law was powerless to do in that it was weakened by the sinful nature, God did by sending his own Son in the likeness of sinful man to be a sin offering. And so he condemned sin in sinful man, in order that the righteous requirements of the law might be fully met in us, who do not live according to the sinful nature but according to the Spirit.

The God of grace (unmerited kindness) became a man so He could redeem us from our wickedness. Jesus fulfilled the requirements of the law and was crucified for us, taking our deserved penalty of death. He then rose again from the dead, proving His victory over sin and the grave. Now we who believe in Christ are united with Him in his death, burial, and resurrection. Because of His completed work, we are declared by God to be holy and are destined to stand spotless and blameless before Him for all time and eternity. God transferred all our sin, including our sexual sins, both known and hidden, onto Jesus. He then transferred all of Jesus' righteousness and holiness to us who have repented and received Jesus as our own Savior. Praise God!

When I served on board Navy ships, many times I had the watch late at night. That meant I had to stay awake for a designated period of time, usually four hours, and perform duties to ensure the safe, smooth operation of the ship. One station on the ship where I stood watch was the bridge, where the ship is controlled and steered. At night no white lights are allowed on the bridge because they would hinder one's ability to look out and see other ships or obstacles to safe navigation. Instead, all the lights and flashlights have a red filter over the lens, maximizing night vision.

Over the course of the watch as the Officer of the Deck, I would receive many messages and have to read many documents. I could read every document as long as it was not written in red ink or red felt-tipped pen. If the document was written in red, the red light would blend with the ink or pencil. This happened to me more than once. Someone would hand me a sheet of paper to sign, but the paper looked blank to me.

This is exactly what the Scriptures teach regarding how God looks upon those who have trusted in His Son as Savior. Isaiah 1:18 says, "Come now, let us reason together. . . . Though your sins are like scarlet, they shall be as white as snow; though they are red as crimson, they shall be like wool." Once we receive Jesus, His red blood acts like the red light on a ship's bridge, and the list of our sins written in the color of sin (red) is covered. So when God looks at us, He no longer sees our sin. Instead He sees us through the filter of His beloved Son, our Savior.

Regardless of how we feel about ourselves and our past sexual sins, God sees us as pure, spotless, holy, and blameless in Christ. We may still be suffering from the effects of our sin, but our standing before Him is secure and unstained.

However, until our time on earth is finished and God takes us home, we will battle to be holy and to keep sexually pure. God is aware of the struggle we face daily. He has made provision for us through His Holy Spirit and has given us examples and guidelines in Scripture as to how to purify ourselves and stay clean.

> *For I do not want you to be ignorant of the fact, brothers, that our forefathers were all under the cloud and that they all passed through the sea. They were all baptized into Moses in the cloud and in the sea. They all ate the same spiritual food and drank the same spiritual drink; for they drank from the spiritual rock that accompanied them, and that rock was Christ. Nevertheless, God was not pleased with most of them; their bodies were scattered over the desert. Now these things occurred as examples, to keep us from setting our hearts on evil things as they did. . . . We should not commit sexual immorality, as some of them did—and in one day twenty-three thousand of them died. . . . These things happened to them as examples and were written down as warnings for us, on whom the fulfillment of the ages has come. So, if you think you are standing firm, be careful that you don't fall! No temptation has seized you except what is common to man. And God is faithful; he will not let you be tempted beyond what you can bear. But when you are tempted, he will also provide a way out so that you can stand up under it.*
>
> *—1 Corinthians 10:1-6, 8, 11-13*

As believers, we must learn to drink from the same "spiritual rock" (Christ) from which the Israelites failed to consistently drink. God delivered them from Egypt, and He has delivered us from the penalty of sin. The children of Israel had to walk before God and live up to His standards while in the Promised Land. Similarly, though we have been set free from our sins by faith in Christ, we must continue to walk by faith and obedience in all areas of our lives. We could not rid ourselves of our sin, and we are equally incapable to live holy, pleasing lives before God without His help. We must live by faith through the power of the indwelling Holy Spirit.

When a large ship enters a harbor, it takes on board a harbor master, a man who knows the harbor, knows where any hazards to navigation are located, and knows the strength and directions of the tides and currents. The harbor master takes control of the ship, giving orders to the helmsman who steers the ship. He is an outside expert to help safely bring the ship to a safe docking.

The harbor master for the believer is the Holy Spirit. He enters our lives at the moment of salvation and seeks to control our minds, wills, and emotions for the glory of the Father. As we learn and apply the Word of God, He will whisper to our consciences and make suggestions to our minds about what to do and what to avoid. If we follow His kind instructions, we will find safety and protection on our journey. Failure to obey the Holy Spirit leads to spiritual disaster.

For years every time I would take a shower, I would masturbate. It was a twenty-year-long practice that I had tried to stop numerous times in my own strength. One day when I was reviewing some Scripture I had memorized, I thought about Romans 8. Verse 13 especially stood out to me as I was again struggling to stop masturbating: "But if by the Spirit you put to death the misdeeds of the body, you will live." I remember thinking, "How can the Spirit interact with my flesh and actually control the evil deeds of my body?" I prayed, "Lord, I don't understand how this works. Please control me; please fill me. I yield to You. Please help me stop masturbating when I take a shower."

I prayed that prayer just prior to taking a shower. The next conscious thought I had, I was fully dressed and walking down the passageway of the USS *Bainbridge*, the ship I was assigned to at that time. I suddenly realized that I had not masturbated! I was amazed. It had been decades since I had not performed this lustful act in the shower. The Holy Spirit had made Romans 8:13 a reality in my life. Somehow the Spirit controlled my thinking so that the thought of masturbating did not enter my mind while I was in the shower. God had showed me a significant truth from the Scriptures!

I prayed that prayer the next day and the day after that with the same success. Through the Spirit's help, the showers ceased to be a stumbling-block for me. If you know the Lord Jesus Christ, the Holy Spirit is available to you also. But you must call upon Him to help you. You must ask.

But there were still other areas of my life that needed help that were not as easy to change. There were many other lessons to learn, truths I was ignorant of, and strongholds that still hindered me in the battle for sexual purity. In this book I will tell you how the Lord has helped me learn to conquer these strongholds in large measure.

KEY PRINCIPLE

Though we have sinned sexually and in other ways, Jesus has paid the price for our sins, and now we can experience victory over lust.

KEY VERSE

"But among you there must not be even a hint of sexual immorality, or of any kind of impurity, or of greed, because these are improper for God's holy people" (Ephesians 5:3).

DISCUSSION QUESTIONS

1. As you consider the types of sexual contact God has prohibited, what seem to be the core issues or principles?

2. Why do you think God clearly laid down so many rules and regulations for this area of our lives? How do people respond generally to these regulations? How do you?

3. "I've heard that to become a follower of Christ, you have to give up all the fun of sex and become like a monk." What is an appropriate biblical response to this statement?

4. What can you specifically do to allow the Spirit to "put to death the misdeeds" of your body? Talk to the Lord about this now.

CHAPTER
THREE
———

The Supreme Battle

God desires to be known by men and women everywhere. He is a loving, holy God who created us and made a way for us to know Him personally.

Early in human history He chose for Himself a person through whom He would bless every nation. Through Abraham and his seed God would form a holy people by which His glory would be made manifest throughout the earth. He gave that nation a unique and glorious set of laws and regulations for living—wonderful principles of holiness and wholeness that His children were to obey with all their hearts, souls, minds, and strength because they loved the Author. God's glory would have been revealed through the blessings He bestowed on His obedient people. However, disobedience would lead to discipline and chastening. Deuteronomy 4:6-8 says:

> Observe them [God's decrees and laws] carefully, for this
> will show your wisdom and understanding to the nations,
> who will hear about all these decrees and say, "Surely this
> great nation is a wise and understanding people." What

other nation is so great as to have their gods near them the
way the LORD our God is near us whenever we pray to him?
And what other nation is so great as to have such righteous
decrees and laws as this body of laws I am setting before you
today?

We know what happened. Israel disobeyed. After Moses and
his generation passed away, the people turned away from God,
every man doing what was right in his own eyes. God raised up
judges to deliver them, but the people persisted in returning to
their disobedience. They forgot about and ignored the God who
created them and went whoring after other gods.

Then God raised up David, a man after His own heart, who
led his people back to God. But even David, a strong man, had a
weak moment and fell into sexual sin. His wife, Bathsheba, bore
him Solomon, who would become a future king with heaven-sent
wisdom. Solomon carried out the vision of David and built a temple for God to dwell in. The purposes of Israel and the people of
God are again seen in Solomon's prayer of dedication of the temple, found in 1 Kings 8:41-43:

> *"As for the foreigner who does not belong to your people*
> *Israel but has come from a distant land because of your*
> *name—for men will hear of your great name and your*
> *mighty hand and your outstretched arm—when he comes*
> *and prays toward this temple, then hear from heaven, your*
> *dwelling place, and do whatever the foreigner asks of you,*
> so that all the peoples of the earth may know your name *and*
> *fear you, as do your own people Israel, and may know that*
> *this house I have built bears your Name." (emphasis mine)*

The glory of the temple was such that people from every
nation would come and seek God there. Israel's temple and the

presence of the glory of the Father would act like a magnet, drawing people to the knowledge of God.

The Queen of Sheba gave testimony to the glory of the temple and to the spreading fame of God. First Kings 10:1, 4, 5, 6, 9 says:

When the queen of Sheba heard about the fame of Solomon and his relation to the name of the LORD, she came to test him with hard questions. . . . When the queen of Sheba saw all the wisdom of Solomon and the palace he had built . . . and the burnt offerings he made at the temple of the LORD, she was overwhelmed. She said to the king, ". . . Praise be to the LORD your God, who has delighted in you and placed you on the throne of Israel. Because of the LORD's eternal love for Israel, he has made you king, to maintain justice and righteousness."

But again the people forgot the decrees of the Lord and sought after other gods. The nation fell into unbelief and the pursuit of idolatry until God again intervened to make Himself known, this time through Elijah. Unbelief had spread so much that at this juncture in history Elijah thought he was the *only* person on the face of the earth who worshiped the one true God: "I am the only one of the Lord's prophets left, but Baal has four hundred and fifty prophets" (1 Kings 18:22). The famous encounter between Elijah and the prophets of Baal then occurred, with fire being called down from heaven.

At the time of sacrifice, the prophet Elijah stepped forward and prayed: "O LORD, God of Abraham, Isaac and Israel, let it be known today that you are God in Israel and that I am your servant and have done all these things at your command. Answer me, O LORD, answer me, so these people will know that you, O LORD, are God, and that you are turning

*their hearts back again." Then the fire of the LORD fell and
burned up the sacrifice, the wood, the stones and the soil,
and also licked up the water in the trench. When all the people saw this, they fell prostrate and cried, "The LORD—he
is God! The LORD—he is God!"*

—1 Kings 18:36-39

What a victory! And yet soon afterwards, the people again
engaged in disobedience. There was a continuing spiritual dete-
rioration nationally. God sent prophets to warn of impending
doom and the coming deportation of the nation, but to no avail.
After God allowed His people to be taken abroad as captives
because of their persistent disobedience, He still found ways of
making His name known through miraculous acts of deliverance,
even using pagan kings to work His will.

For example, He intervened in the lives of his believing servants Shadrach, Meshach, and Abednego, delivering them from
the fiery furnace of the mighty Babylonian king. Nebuchad-
nezzar, after seeing four, not three, men in the furnace, said
(Daniel 3:28):

*"Praise be to the God of Shadrach, Meshach and Abed-
nego, who has sent his angel and rescued his servants! They
trusted in him and defied the king's command and were willing to give up their lives rather than serve or worship any
god except their own God. Therefore I decree that the people of any nation or language who say anything against the
God of Shadrach, Meshach and Abednego be cut into pieces
and their houses be turned into piles of rubble, for no other
god can save in this way." (emphasis mine)*

This same book later records another miraculous intervention
of God in the life of one of his faithful servants. Daniel was tossed

into the lions' den because he violated the laws of the state by praying to God. When he was not eaten by the lions, King Darius expressed his gratitude to the true God by issuing the following decree, found in Daniel 6:26-27:

> *"I issue a decree that in every part of my kingdom people must fear and reverence the God of Daniel. For he is the living God and he endures forever; his kingdom will not be destroyed, his dominion will never end. He rescues and he saves; he performs signs and wonders in the heavens and on the earth. He has rescued Daniel from the power of the lions."*

It is important to note that Daniel and his three friends were holy men. Daniel 1 tells us they purposed not to defile themselves with the king's food (foods forbidden by God's laws for the people of Israel). God intervened and helped them to keep their pledge and to keep pure dietarily. As a result of their faithfulness, God used them to bring about the proclamations of pagan kings to make His name known.

But after all the miracles, all the warnings, all the prophets and messengers, Israel still did not understand the purposes of God. Finally, in His clearest and most dramatic move yet, the Son of God became a man—Jesus. His purposes on earth were very clear. In His prayer found in John 17 He pled:

> *"I have brought you glory on earth by completing the work you gave me to do. . . . I have revealed you to those whom you gave me out of the world . . . and they believed that you sent me. . . . As you have sent me into the world, I have sent them into the world. . . . I pray also for those who will believe in me through their message."*
>
> *—Verses 4, 6, 8, 18, 20*

Jesus announced, "The Son of Man came to seek and to save what was lost" (Luke 19:10). He chose twelve disciples to be with Him and sent them forth to preach. He has given His followers a special commission: "Therefore go and make disciples of all nations . . ." (Matthew 28:19-20). God still has a heart for the nations and desires to reach them. He wants every person in the world to learn about and know Him, and He primarily accomplishes this through His holy people. He could use a talking donkey, as he has in the past (Numbers 22:21-35). He could spread the Word through rocks crying out (Luke 19:40) or through the use of angelic messengers (see, for example, Matthew 28:2-7; Mark 16:1-8; Luke 1:8-20, 26-38; 2:8-15; 24:1-8). But He desires to use His own people. First Peter 2:9-11 tells us:

> *But you are a chosen people, a royal priesthood, a holy nation, a people belonging to God,* that you may declare the praises of him who called you out of darkness into his wonderful light. *Once you were not a people, but now you are the people of God; once you had not received mercy, but now you have received mercy. Dear friends, I urge you, as aliens and strangers in the world, to abstain from sinful desires, which war against your soul. (emphasis mine)*

It is clear from this passage that God wants to use His redeemed, holy people to proclaim His Word to the rest of the world. But to be able to be used in this way, we must fight to keep pure, resisting evil impulses that attack our souls. Second Timothy 2:19-22 confirms this premise:

> *"Everyone who confesses the name of the Lord must turn away from wickedness." In a large house there are articles not only of gold and silver, but also of wood and clay; some*

are for noble purposes and some for ignoble. If a man cleanses himself from the latter, he will be an instrument for noble purposes, made holy, useful to the Master *and prepared to do any good work. Flee the evil desires of youth.* . . . *(emphasis mine)*

Unholiness leads to uselessness in God's kingdom. It always has, and it always will.

Jesus warned about us this in Matthew 5:13: "You are the salt of the earth. But if the salt loses its saltiness, how can it be made salty again? It is no longer good for anything, except to be thrown out and trampled by men." He also warned about fruitlessness in John 15:2, 6: "He cuts off every branch in me that bears no fruit, while every branch that does bear fruit he prunes so that it will be even more fruitful. . . . If anyone does not remain in me, he is like a branch that is thrown away and withers; such branches are picked up, thrown into the fire and burned." He is not talking about the loss of salvation but about usefulness or uselessness in the kingdom.

Once a country starts a war, it must continue building war-making equipment—tanks, planes, ships, etc.—to replenish what has been destroyed and to strengthen any gains made in the war effort. During World War II as the Japanese continued their ship-building program, hundreds of designers, naval architects, welders, and craftsmen set about to build the largest aircraft carrier ever constructed, the *Shinano*. Thousands of man-hours went into the design and construction of that warship. They did all they could to make that war vessel useful and effective. Obviously, they didn't build it to have it sink before it got into battle, and yet this is precisely what happened!

In 1940 the Japanese had laid the keel for the *Shinano*, originally intending for the vessel to be a battleship. After several years of construction, they decided to convert it to an aircraft carrier, retaining the battleship hull. Four Japanese aircraft carriers had been sunk at Midway, so this new ship was meant to withstand any attack. The flight deck was made of steel almost twelve inches thick. This deck lay atop a thick layer of concrete. Since no amount of traditional bombardment could substantially damage her, the commanding officer concluded the *Shinano* was unsinkable.

On November 18, 1944, the *Shinano* was commissioned, though she was not yet ready for battle. Her crew had to be trained, and much additional equipment needed to be placed on board, including rubber gaskets for the watertight doors. Failure to have such a gasket makes watertight doors useless. Ten days after commissioning, the *Shinano* left its berth and headed for the Inland Sea, where final touches would be added. She was escorted by three Japanese destroyers.

American submarines had been operating in that area. One of those submarines, the USS *Archerfish*, made radar contact with the *Shinano* only two hours after the aircraft carrier had been at sea. Closing rapidly at about twenty knots, the *Archerfish* fired six torpedoes at the *Shinano* from about 1,400 yards away. Four of the six exploded. The commanding officer of the *Shinano*, believing his ship was unsinkable, continued on the same course and speed for the next eight hours. Meanwhile, flooding was occurring through all the doors and hatches, none of which had yet been made watertight. The crew was inexperienced, discipline broke down, and the morale of the men failed. The loss of the ship was inevitable.

The *Shinano* sank just ten days after being commissioned, taking most of her crew to their death. The *Shinano* never fired a shot, never contributed to the war effort, never had a chance to function in the way she was designed. The *Shinano* was the largest but shortest-lived warship in history.

The *Shinano* sank because the doors and hatches were not watertight. Modern ship construction calls for dividing a ship into hundreds of watertight compartments. The theory is that if one watertight compartment or room takes on water, the water will not spread to other rooms. Thus a large surface ship could receive numerous torpedo hits or bombs in and around the hull and still not sink—that is, if all the doors and hatches are properly secured and well maintained. On U.S. Navy ships, every door, hatch, and scuttle is labeled with a code, whether X (X-ray), Y (Yoke), or Z (Zebra). At certain times of the day and in certain battle conditions, some or all of the doors are securely shut. When enemy attack is imminent, Condition Zebra is set—all X, Y, and Z doors are quickly shut, providing the maximum amount of watertight integrity for the ship. Sailors are dispatched throughout the entire ship to ensure that the thousands of doors, hatches, and scuttles are shut. Reports are brought back to the Damage Control Officer, who is responsible to train all personnel to fight fires and stop flooding and keep the ship afloat if damaged in war.

As Christians, we must guard the doors and hatches into our souls. Just as men in the Navy set watch over every opening that could allow water into the ship, we must set a vigilant watch over our eyes, ears, and minds so we do not become defiled by the world. "The eye is the lamp of the body. If your eyes are good, your whole body will be full of light. But if your eyes are bad, your whole body will be full of darkness. If then the light within you is darkness, how great is that darkness!" (Matthew 6:22-23).

Holiness is to a Christian what watertight integrity is to a ship. It is indispensable. But the goal of a warship is not merely to keep water out of its hull. Its purpose is to get into the war and fight and work for victory. Failure to get into the battle renders the ship worthless to the nation that built it, and the failure of a believer to get into the battle for the souls of men renders the believer useless. A believer must involve himself in the warfare to which the Father has called him.

We must fight a battle for sexual purity, seeking to be more and more like Jesus. First John 3:1 says, "Dear friends, now we are children of God, and what we will be has not yet been made known. But we know that when he appears, we shall be like him, for we shall see him as he is. Everyone who has this hope in him purifies himself, just as he is pure." If we want to be useful to God in the harvest of lost souls, we must be sexually pure.

Jesus said He came "to seek and to save" the "lost"—those who have not put their faith in Jesus Christ and so have not received forgiveness of sin. The life pursuit of Jesus was to train laborers for the harvest and to send them out to do what the Father had sent Jesus to do—to win the lost. To the extent that we are engaged in the same struggle as Jesus, we are fighting the one war worthy of all our energy. As Paul said, "We proclaim him, admonishing and teaching everyone with all wisdom, so that we may present everyone perfect in Christ. To this end I labor, struggling with all his energy, which so powerfully works in me" (Colossians 1:28-29).

God is training and developing us to become more and more like Jesus in character and in purpose. God desires to use us in His harvest fields, exerting all our efforts to introduce Him to those who do not know Him. He desires us to do this with the same methodology and character as His Son. The battle for sexual purity must be fought and won so that we may be ready to serve God in the fight for the souls of men, women, and children. When God's people live unholy lifestyles, they render themselves useless to God; they become defiled.

First Corinthians 6:18 says, "Flee from sexual immorality. All other sins a man commits are outside his body, but he who sins sexually sins against his own body." In Navy terminology, "scuttling a ship" means that its own crew sinks the ship. Sexual sin by a Christian is an act of scuttling oneself from the battle for men's souls, rendering ourselves unusable to a holy God. A ship is designed to float *on* the water, but water *inside* the ship is deadly.

We live in a sex-filled, sex-saturated world. In contrast, God has set up standards of holiness and right living regarding sexual conduct and thought. Violating these standards will shipwreck our faith. The enemy wins another battle whenever he sinks a Christian before he even gets into the battle, reminiscent of the *Shinano*.

We cannot hope to speak effectively or truly for our Lord if we are not obeying Him in regard to our lives sexually. Obedience is essential!

KEY PRINCIPLE

To effectively proclaim God's love and win others to Christ, we must be sexually pure.

KEY VERSES

"But you are a chosen people, a royal priesthood, a holy nation, a people belonging to God, that you may declare the praises of

him who called you out of darkness into his wonderful light. Once
you were not a people, but now you are the people of God; once
you had not received mercy, but now you have received mercy.
Dear friends, I urge you, as aliens and strangers in the world,
to abstain from sinful desires, which war against your soul"
(1 Peter 2:9-11).

DISCUSSION QUESTIONS

1. Do you agree or disagree that the supreme battle for the
believer is the battle for the souls of men? Why? What importance does this matter have in your life?

2. Evaluate how you are doing at guarding your eyes, ears, and
thought life. Practically, how are you protecting yourself in these
areas?

3. Do you agree or disagree with the connection between usefulness and fruitfulness? Why or why not? In what ways would
you like to be more fruitful?

CHAPTER FOUR

Dead to Sin—
Alive to God

During my career in the Navy, I served on various ships. My first ship was the USS *Enterprise*, a nuclear-powered aircraft carrier. That ship is almost a quarter of a mile long and displaces close to 100,000 tons fully loaded. To build an aircraft carrier in peacetime can take two to four years, depending on labor disputes, budget wranglings, changing specifications from the Navy, etc. Once the keel is laid, it takes thousands of tons of steel welded together to construct the ship. While the ship is being built, it stays in dry dock the whole time.

As the ship is being built, the entire steel structure takes on the magnetic signature of the earth. Having a north pole and a south pole, magnetic lines of flux run through the entire earth. In the steel structure of any ship, the steel molecules align themselves according to these magnetic forces, in essence making the ship a large magnet.

This has serious implications in time of war. When a vessel approaches a mine that is activated by a slight change in the magnetic field, the ship itself detonates the explosive charge. In such a situation the seeds of a ship's destruction lie within the ship itself.

Knowing these things about warfare and the nature of ships, the Navy wisely puts the ship through several processes to try to avoid such a catastrophe. In one of these processes, the Navy places coils of wire on the hull of the ship and runs an electric current through those coils. This in essence creates a large electromagnetic field that masks the magnetic signature of the vessel. Theoretically, the magnetic mine would then not explode.

Just as a ship has within it a signature that could lead to destruction, within me is a natural desire to sin, which is deadly to the soul. Paul refers to this in Romans 7:21-25:

> So I find this law at work: When I want to do good, evil is right there with me. For in my inner being I delight in God's law; but I see another law at work in the members of my body, waging war against the law of my mind and making me a prisoner of the law of sin at work within my members. What a wretched man I am! Who will rescue me from this body of death? Thanks be to God—through Jesus Christ our Lord! So then, I myself in my mind am a slave to God's law, but in the sinful nature a slave to the law of sin.

God revealed this truth to me during a time when I was struggling with pornography. I was feeling trapped, as if I were in a spider's web, unable to free myself from my desires and the shameful habit of looking at pornography. I was feeling dirty, stained, powerless, unforgiven, and unforgivable. I felt ashamed and unqualified to be God's child. After running through my mental list of things I had learned about my struggle, I came up empty. Why was I lusting in this trap of pornography again? I could feel my spiritual strength slipping away. I felt like I was dying spiritu-

ally—alienated from God and alone. I was reaching a point of
desperation, crying out day and night for wisdom and understanding. I knew I needed help, and yet I had no desire to read the
Word or to pray. "Lord, please rescue me" was all I could pray.

My wife had picked up Charles Colson's book *Loving God*.
She was really enjoying it and recommended it to me. God used
a section of that book (beginning with page 118) to open my eyes
to what was going on inside me.

> After my conversion, I sat in prison reading from
> Augustine's *Confessions* the well-known story of his youth-
> ful escapade of stealing pears from a neighbor's tree.
> Augustine recorded that late one night a group of youngsters
> went out to "shake down and rob this tree. We took great
> loads of fruit from it, not for our own eating but rather to
> throw it to the pigs." He went on to berate himself for the
> depth of sin this revealed. "The fruit I gathered I threw away,
> devouring in it only iniquity. There was no other reason, but
> foul was the evil and I loved it." Contemporary critics,
> though generous in their praise of Augustine's literary
> genius and profound philosophical insights, mock him for
> his seeming obsession with the pear tree episode. Why
> would one harmless prank loom so large in the saint's mind?
> By his own admission he had taken a mistress, fathered a
> child out of wedlock, and indulged in every fleshly passion.
> Surely any of these were more serious than stealing pears.
> But Augustine saw in the pear incident his true nature and
> the nature of all mankind: in each of us there is sin—not just
> susceptibility to sin, but sin itself. Augustine's love for sen-
> sual pleasure could be explained as the natural arousing of
> his human desires, proving inner weakness or susceptibility
> to sinning. But he had stolen those pears for the pure enjoy-
> ment of stealing (he had an abundance of better pears on his
> own trees). Augustine knew his act was more than weak-
> ness; it was sin itself—sin for the sake of sinning.

The solution for me was similar to that of the ship. Instead of electrical wire wrapped around me with a current flowing through it, I am to "clothe [myself] with the Lord Jesus Christ, and . . . not think about how to gratify the desires of the sinful nature" (Romans 13:14). To the extent that I put on Jesus, I put off the flesh. The more that Jesus is preeminent in my thinking, the less lust will drive or control me. The more that I reckon myself dead to sin, the more I reckon myself alive to God.

But how do I put on the Lord Jesus Christ? First of all, this is an act of the will. I must choose to put Him on. I find it helpful to run through a mental checklist of questions to monitor my spiritual state. When was the last time I spent quality time reading the Bible? When was the last time I memorized a Bible passage? When was the last time I thought about a passage from the Bible? How is my devotional life? When was the last time I shared the Gospel with someone? When was the last time I had a meaningful time of prayer? When was the last time I truly worshiped the Lord? How is my relationship with my close Christian brothers? When was the last time I allowed someone to show their love for me by rebuking me? When was the last time I asked to be filled with the Spirit? These and other questions pinpoint the quality of my relationship with the Lord.

I put on the Lord Jesus Christ when I choose to be filled with the Holy Spirit. I put on the Lord Jesus Christ when I choose to die to myself and obey His commands.

Charles Colson's book made me acutely aware that the reason I was struggling with pornography was because I enjoy sexual sin. My flesh loves lust; I love to sin. This wasn't a brand-new thought. I'd been aware of this state of affairs in myself before. Hebrews 3:13 says, "But encourage one another daily, as long as it is called Today, so that none of you may be hardened by sin's deceitfulness." I had slipped again into a state of the hardening of my spiritual arteries through neglect of the disciplines of the Christian life. I had yielded to sensuality. Romans 6:16 says, "Don't you know that when you offer yourselves to someone to obey him as slaves, you are slaves to the one whom you obey— whether you are slaves to sin, which leads to death, or to obedience, which leads to righteousness?" I had yielded myself to sensuality, and now I was again its slave.

What is the solution when the source of temptation is our own flesh? God made us sexual beings. Our body loves sexual experience by His design. Sex is healthy and normal and holy within the guidelines He has established. But how do we keep these natural drives and urges in check? The God-given solution is to *reckon ourselves dead to sin*. Romans 6:1-14 says:

What shall we say, then? Shall we go on sinning so that grace may increase? By no means! We died to sin; how can we live in it any longer? Or don't you know that all of us who were baptized into Christ Jesus were baptized into his death? We were therefore buried with him through baptism into death in order that, just as Christ was raised from the dead through the glory of the Father, we too may live a new life. If we have been united with him like this in his death, we will certainly also be united with him in his resurrection. For we know that our old self was crucified with him so that the body of sin might be done away with, that we should no longer be slaves to sin—because anyone who has died has been freed from sin. Now if we died with Christ, we believe that we will also live with him. For we know that since Christ was raised from the dead, he cannot die again; death no longer has mastery over him. The death he died, he died to sin once for all; but the life he lives, he lives to God. In the same way, count yourselves dead to sin but alive to God in Christ Jesus. Therefore do not let sin reign in your mortal body so that you obey its evil desires. Do not offer the parts of your body to sin, as instruments of wickedness, but rather offer yourselves to God, as those who have been brought from death to life; and offer the parts of your body to him as instruments of righteousness. For sin shall not be your master, because you are not under law, but under grace.

Have you ever been praying when suddenly your mind is filled with garbage? Or have you ever been reading or studying the Bible when from out of nowhere you start to see in your mind an erotic scene from a movie or a flashback from a life experience you had tried to forget? When I recognize the source of the temptation as my own flesh, I run to Romans 6 and start considering myself dead to sin. I have memorized that whole chapter, and I strongly urge you to do the same. When the attack occurs, I start remembering, picturing, and personalizing Romans 6.

What then, shall I, Bob Daniels, continue to think lustful (personalize this, naming your sin—immoral or homosexual or adulterous or . . .) thoughts that grace may increase? By no means. How can I who died to lustful thoughts still live in them? Do I not know that I have been baptized with Christ Jesus and that I was baptized into his death? I was buried therefore with Him by baptism into death.

At this point I actually picture Jesus on the cross—not the bloodless Jesus the modern-day artists depict, but the picture of Jesus in Isaiah 52:14—"his appearance was so disfigured beyond that of any man and his form marred beyond human likeness." I see Jesus with blood flowing over His whole face, blood dripping down His hands and arms. I see the open wound in His side where blood and water flowed out. I see His bloody, bruised back. I see the crown of thorns piercing His skin. I see the form of a man who is gaunt, pale, exhausted as He hangs there for me. In my mind's eye, I then picture how I would look if I were on that cross. I put a crown on my head. I see the blood dripping down my face, the spikes in my hands and feet, the spear wound in my side. I see myself dead, hanging on the cross.

Romans 6:11 says, "In the same way, count yourselves dead to sin but alive to God in Christ Jesus." When I go through this mental scenario, the impure thoughts flee. I seldom get past verse 2 or 3 of Romans 6 without regaining control of my thought life. This is my battle plan to fight against my own fleshly desires. I may have to go through the first part of Romans 6 several times if the attack is particularly strong, but I've found God's promises to be true again and again.

I realize that not everyone is comfortable with a picturing process, and that there are forms of visualization, New-Age and otherwise, that should be avoided by all of us. However, the use of our imagination in a valid, God-honoring way can be helpful. I am not presenting this as a good practice for everyone. I am simply saying this is one way I reckon myself dead to sin and free from its lure or hold.

I know action such as this takes great effort. It may seem not to work initially, but if you persist it will bring victory. Cry out to God as you recite Romans 6. Apply James 4:7 as well: "Submit yourselves, then, to God. Resist the devil, and he will flee from you." This is not wishful thinking but a promise from God, and not only a promise but a weapon we are to employ in our battle for purity. Ephesians 6:11-17 says: ·

*Put on the full armor of God so that you can take your stand
against the devil's schemes. For our struggle is not against
flesh and blood, but against the rulers, against the author-
ities, against the powers of this dark world and against the
spiritual forces of evil in the heavenly realms. Therefore put
on the full armor of God, so that when the day of evil comes,
you may be able to stand your ground, and after you have
done everything, to stand. Stand firm then, with the belt of
truth buckled around your waist, with the breastplate of
righteousness in place, and with your feet fitted with the
readiness that comes from the gospel of peace. In addition
to all this, take up the shield of faith, with which you can
extinguish all the flaming arrows of the evil one. Take the
helmet of salvation and the sword of the Spirit, which is the
word of God.*

When we consider ourselves dead to sin, we are utilizing spiritual tools the Lord has mercifully provided for us. *Reckoning* is
one of the main weapons the Lord has given us for the battle for
sexual purity. We must use this weapon or suffer defeat at the
hands of our own flesh.

KEY PRINCIPLE

*The more I put on Christ, the less lust will overpower me; the
more I reckon myself dead to sin, the more I will be the man God
wants me to be.*

KEY VERSES

*"For we know that since Christ was raised from the dead, he can-
not die again; death no longer has mastery over him. The death*

he died, he died to sin once for all; but the life he lives, he lives to God. In the same way, count yourselves dead to sin but alive to God in Christ Jesus. Therefore do not let sin reign in your mortal body so that you obey its evil desires" (Romans 6:9-12).

DISCUSSION QUESTIONS

1. What does it mean to put on the Lord Jesus Christ? How do you do this practically? Is this a consistent reality in your life? Why or why not?

2. What does it mean to reckon yourself dead to sin? How do you do this practically? Is this a consistent reality in your life? Why or why not?

3. What pieces of the armor of God do you use most consistently? What pieces are most lacking? What can you do to be better armed in the battle for sexual purity day by day? Talk to God about this right now.

CHAPTER FIVE

Protected by the Promises of God

Imagine sitting on a warship and putting your hand against the wall ("bulkhead" in Navy language) of a ship. Now hold your hands twenty-four inches apart. That is how thick some of the walls were on older battleships. In fact, the armor plating on an American battleship is so thick that a Russian Styx missile would bounce off an armor-plated bulkhead on a direct hit. You would probably feel pretty secure behind such walls of defense.

Armor on a ship is placed in areas where the ship is the most vulnerable to enemy projectiles. Normally, an armor belt is placed around the sides of the ship from about ten feet below the waterline to just above the waterline. Theoretically, a torpedo hitting the armor belt would not penetrate into the hull and cause flooding. Similarly, armor plating would be placed along the upper surface of the ship to repel bombs dropped from airplanes.

God has given us armor for protection and victory, invaluable in our struggle to live holy lives. This armor consists of the power and promises of God at work within us. Second Peter 1:3-4 says, "His divine power has given us everything we need for life and godliness through our knowledge of him who called us by his own glory and goodness. Through these he has given us his very great and precious promises, so that through them you may participate in the divine nature and escape the corruption in the world caused by evil desires." Ephesians 6:16 adds, "Take up the shield of faith, with which you can extinguish all the flaming arrows of the evil one."

To the extent that a believer knows, believes, claims, and lives by the promises of God, he displays spiritual maturity and experiences moral victory. Everything in the Christian life is based on something God has promised His children. He promises us eternal life if we believe in His Son (John 3:36). He promises to reward us for our faith (Hebrews 11:6). He promises us that He'll never leave us or forsake us (Matthew 28:20; Hebrews 13:5). He promises us that someday we'll receive new bodies (Philippians 3:21). He promises us power for fruitful witness (Acts 1:8). He promises to answer our prayers (Matthew 7:7-8). His promises to us cannot be counted.

In the struggle for sexual purity, just as in every other area of the Christian life and struggle, God's promises are foundational. They are real, and they are given though we do not deserve them. But they must be claimed and acted on; otherwise they are like uncashed checks. Heaven's promises are swords in the battle for purity. Many times we have to hold on to God's promises and cling to them regardless of how we feel. Ephesians 6:13 says, "Therefore put on the full armor of God, so that when the day of evil comes, you may be able to stand your ground, and after you have done everything, to stand." If we leave the battlefield still standing, we've won!

Believe the promises, and not your feelings, not the messages your flesh is telling you, not the accusations of the evil one. Second Corinthians 10:5 says, "We take captive every thought to make it obedient to Christ." I have too often believed lies about myself, others, and even God. These lies always started in the form of isolated thoughts that eventually became patterns of thinking. At such times we must "take captive" lying thoughts and choose to believe God's truth. Here we see another key principle in the battle for sexual purity: "the truth will set you free" (John 8:32).

My good friend Dick Stiliha gave me the chart seen below, listing some of the messages that we believe or tell ourselves and what God says about us. The dilemma we face is the same that Eve faced in the Garden of Eden. She had to choose between what God said and what Satan said, and we face the same choice today. I challenge you, as my friend challenged me, to look at what you feel or think about yourself from column 1, then see what God says about you in column 2. Each day take one of the truths from column 2 and confess out loud what God says, meditate or think about it for awhile, then write down your thoughts about His promises. In this way you can take control of your thoughts.

OLD LIFE (Lies)—Channel 1	NEW LIFE (Truth)—Channel 2
What I think or feel about myself	*What is true about me*
1. I am unworthy/unacceptable.	I am accepted and worthy. *Psalm 139:13-24* *Romans 15:7*
2. I feel like a failure/inadequate.	I am adequate. *2 Corinthians 3:5-6* *Philippians 4:13*
3. I am a fearful/anxious person.	I am free from fear. *Psalm 34:4; 2 Timothy 1:7; 1 Peter 5:7; 1 John 4:18*

4. I am a weak person.

I am strong in Christ.
Psalm 37:34; Daniel 11:32;
Philippians 4:19

5. I am in bondage.

I am free.
Psalm 32:7; John 8:36;
2 Corinthians 3:17

6. I'm not very smart.

I have God's wisdom.
Proverbs 2:6-7;
1 Corinthians 1:30; James 1:5

7. I am unloved.

I am very loved.
John 15:9; Romans 8:35-39;
Ephesians 2:4; 5:1;
1 John 4:10-11

8. I am unwanted or
I don't belong to anyone.

I have been adopted by God
and am His child.
Romans 8:15-17; Galatians 4:5-
7; Ephesians 1:5; 1 John 3:2

9. I feel guilty.

I am totally forgiven.
Psalm 103:12; Ephesians 1:7;
Colossians 1:14, 20;
Hebrews 10:17

10. I am depressed and hopeless.

I have all the hope I need.
Psalm 16:11; 27:13; 31:24;
Romans 15:13

11. There is nothing special
about me.

I have been chosen,
set apart by God.
Psalm 139:1; 1 Corinthians
1:30; 6:11; Hebrews 10:10, 14

12. I am not good enough.

I am perfect in Christ.
Colossians 2:13;
Hebrews 10:14

13. I am defeated.

I am victorious.
Romans 8:37; 2 Corinthians
2:14; 1 John 5:4

14. I have no strength.	I have God's power; I am indwelt by the Holy Spirit. *Acts 1:8; Romans 8:9, 11; Ephesians 1:19; 3:16*
15. I feel condemned.	I am blameless. *John 3:18; Romans 8:1*
16. I am alone.	I am never alone. *Romans 8:38-39; Hebrews 13:5*
17. I have no one to take care of me.	I am protected, safe. *Psalm 27:1-6; 32:7-11; 41*
18. I can't reach God.	I have access to God. *Matthew 7:7-8; Ephesians 2:6; 1 Peter 2:5, 9*
19. I am afraid of Satan.	I have authority over Satan. *Colossians 1:13; 1 John 4:4; Revelation 12:7-11*
20. I have no confidence.	I have all the confidence I need. *Proverbs 3:26; 14:26; 28:1; Ephesians 3:12; Hebrews 10:19-22*

Look again at 2 Peter 1:3-4—"His divine power has given us everything we need for life and godliness through our knowledge of him who called us by his own glory and goodness. Through these he has given us his very great and precious promises, so that through them you may participate in the divine nature and escape the corruption in the world caused by evil desires." Focus on these truths as you struggle to maintain purity. Maybe you're ready to quit. Maybe you've fallen into sexual sin and have contracted a disease for which there is no cure. Maybe your shame is so great that you believe you are beyond God's forgiveness or His love and care.

Take courage! God has promised to meet all those needs. You will never advance in your battle for sexual purity until you are ready to believe and receive the promises God has given us in His Word.

Many of us can't count the immoral magazines we've looked at, the objectionable movies we've watched, the pornographic photos we've lusted over. But we are not doomed to ongoing failure. As Psalm 40:11-12 says, "My only hope is in your love and faithfulness. Otherwise I perish, for problems far too big for me to solve are piled higher than my head. Meanwhile *my sins, too many to count*, have all caught up with me and I am ashamed to look up" (*Living Bible*, emphasis mine). Psalm 130:3 adds, "If Thou, Lord, shouldst mark iniquities, O Lord, who could stand?" (*Revised Standard Version*). The authors of the Psalms understood men like me. Truly our sins are without number concerning the many women we've lusted after.

Jesus warned us, "But I tell you that anyone who looks at a woman lustfully has already committed adultery with her in his heart" (Matthew 5:28). Jesus raised the standard of purity above the customary human standards of his day, and especially above the acceptable standards of our day when anything goes sexually, or so men claim. Acutely aware of my own sinfulness, many times I've wondered if God still loves me; since I've sinned more than seventy times seventy, maybe God's well of forgiveness has run dry. I have even thought that maybe it's time for God to take me off this earth so I won't continue to give in to sin and discredit His name.

Several years ago I had torn cartilage in my right knee. Because I was struggling with pornography at the time, I thought maybe this was God's way of disciplining me. As I went into surgery, I feared that God would take me home and I would never see my family again. That's how defeated I felt in my personal battle for purity. After sinning by looking at pornography, I would often be so overcome with guilt that I felt like giving in and abandoning all claims to even be a Christian. I have at times asked God to take away my sex drive—to do whatever it takes to bring these desires raging inside me under control.

David said in Psalm 3:5, "I lie down and sleep; I wake again, because the LORD sustains me." I was sometimes amazed that I woke up in the morning, that I was still alive! I knew the only reason was because the Lord Himself had sustained me. Lamentations 3:22-23 states, "Because of the LORD's great love we are not consumed, for his compassions never fail. They are new every morning; great is your faithfulness." I was grateful that God continued to love me and gave me a new supply of mercy each day. I often found new hope and extra strength from God's promises given in His holy Word.

Another promise I have claimed over and over is 1 John 1:9—"If we confess our sins, he is faithful and just and will forgive us our sins and purify us from all unrighteousness." I've heard this verse called the Christian's bar of soap. We need to request and receive God's gracious cleansing as many times as necessary—whenever our souls and bodies are soiled by sin.

To again quote 2 Peter 1:3-4, "His divine power has given us everything we need for life and godliness through our knowledge of him who called us by his own glory and goodness. Through these *he has given us his very great and precious promises, so that through them you may participate in the divine nature and escape the corruption in the world caused by evil desires*" (emphasis mine). By nature God is a God of holiness, and He desires that we share in His holiness. The promises I have quoted are just a few of the marvelous and exceeding riches we can claim and lean on as we seek to please God by becoming more and more pure in our walk with Him.

KEY PRINCIPLE

Conscious dependence on God's promises protects us from our enemy's attacks and brings us moral victory.

KEY VERSES

"His divine power has given us everything we need for life and godliness through our knowledge of him who called us by his own glory and goodness. Through these he has given us his very great and precious promises, so that through them you may participate in the divine nature and escape the corruption in the world caused by evil desires" (2 Peter 1:3-4).

DISCUSSION QUESTIONS

1. What Bible promises are you claiming in your walk with God? How do these specific promises help you in your battle for sexual purity?

2. Which of God's promises do you find difficult to believe? Why? Is there some fellow Christian whom you respect and with whom you could talk about this?

3. Do you feel you will eventually be able to live a pure live, with God's help? Why or why not? What can you do today, tomorrow, next week to experience more consistent victory in this area of your life?

His Word
In My Heart

On May 26, 1941, a strange event occurred in the history of German submarine U-566, having a profound impact on the course of World War II. The commanding officer of the U-566 was a Lieutenant Wohlfarth. His U-boat was returning from successfully sinking British merchant ships when a lookout sighted two large warships on the horizon, necessitating a crash dive. When they resurfaced a bit later, a quick sweep of the periscope revealed what every wartime submarine skipper dreams of. They were exactly between the two enemy warships. In front of U-566 was the British battle cruiser *Renown*, and to their stern was the British aircraft carrier *Ark Royal*. Wohlfarth could see biplanes on the *Ark Royal* warming their engines, nearly ready for takeoff. U-566 was in perfect position between the two ships. All Wohlfarth had to do was fire torpedoes from both ends and both British ships would be severely damaged, if not sunk. The only problem was, *U-566 had no more torpedoes*! She had used them all during the mission.

Little did Lieutenant Wohlfarth know that one of the planes he had seen warming up on the flight deck of the *Ark Royal* would drop a bomb an hour later that would damage a famous German battleship's rudders. The *Bismarck*, unable to maneuver because of its dysfunctional rudders, then became a sitting duck for the British Navy to pound and eventually sink the next day. Only 118 of the 2,400 men of the *Bismarck* would survive. If U-566 had had more torpedoes . . .

When the USS *Bainbridge*, aboard which I then served, deployed for a Western Pacific cruise in the early eighties, all four missile launchers were operational. We could fire missiles at the enemy four different ways. If one broke down, we had three others to use. That could not be said of all our battleships at that time, since the Navy did not have enough money to keep all ships fully operational. But the enemy didn't know that. We were bluffing by sending out ships with broken missile launchers or an incomplete supply of missiles. The bluff would be discovered only if an enemy attacked an ill-equipped ship. Luckily for the U.S. Navy, no attacks occurred.

Sadly, thousands of followers of Christ find themselves on spiritual battlefronts in the same straits as ships with non-operational missile launchers or with no missiles to fire at the enemy. As believers, our missiles are truths from the Word of God hidden within our hearts, ready for recall at a second's notice when under attack. Ephesians 6:17 says, "Take the helmet of salvation and the sword of the Spirit, which is the word of God."

One of the first Bible passages I ever memorized was Psalm 119:9, 11: "How can a young man keep his way pure? By living according to your word. . . . I have hidden your word in my heart that I might not sin against you." As I interacted with these Scriptures, I thought, how do you first become pure so you can "keep" pure?

Scripture teaches that when we put our faith and trust in the

Lord Jesus Christ as our Savior, from that point on God considers us clean and pure. We are then destined to stand before Him holy, spotless, and blameless. Colossians 1:21-22 says, "Once you were alienated from God and were enemies in your minds because of your evil behavior. But now he has reconciled you by Christ's physical body through death to present you holy in his sight, without blemish and free from accusation."

But how can I "keep [my] way pure," as Psalm 119:11 says? To maintain purity of thought and action, I must regularly and systematically hide God's Word in my heart—I must memorize Scripture. When I am actively engaging my mind in the process of memorization of the Word, my desire for impure things decreases. Conversely, if I am desiring impurity, my personal time in the Word, and particularly Scripture memorization, diminishes. Why is this so?

Several years ago developers in upstate New York built a housing development called Love Canal. Several years later, the families who moved into those houses started experiencing horrible birth defects and diseases. After much legal action and medical investigation, it was discovered that Love Canal was a former toxic waste dumping site. Eventually the state of New York moved all those families out of the houses, condemned the whole area, and posted signs forbidding entry. They even posted a guard to keep the public away from the damaging toxins.

Jeremiah 17:9 says, "The heart is deceitful above all things and beyond cure. Who can understand it?" And Jesus said in Matthew 15:19, " For out of the heart come evil thoughts, murder, adultery, sexual immorality, theft, false testimony, slander." Every person carries within himself his own private toxic waste dump. From this dump site comes the inner desire for sexual sin as well as other acts of disobedience. Just as the government wisely posted guards around Love Canal, God has commanded us to post a guard around our hearts—Scripture memorization coupled with the desire to meditate, understand, and apply the Word in our lives. "How can a young man keep his way pure? By living according to your word" (Psalm 119:9).

Anyone who has stood watch in the Navy knows that normally the maximum time you stand at your post is four to six hours. Any longer than that and the guard becomes too tired to effectively carry out his duties. He needs rest and nourishment along the way. I find the same thing is true regarding Scripture memory. For me, if I go a week or more without memorizing or reflecting on a new or different verse, impure thoughts start manifesting themselves. "I have hidden your word in my heart that I might not sin against you" (Psalm 119:11).

This is another time that a friend or a group of friends can render invaluable support. Left to myself, I get lazy and slothful. I need buddies of like mind who are themselves actively involved in Scripture memory and who will challenge me to press on in the work of Bible memorization—men who are hiding the Scriptures in their own hearts and who will ask me, "What are you memorizing these days, Bob?" In the Appendix I've included a list of Scriptures that have helped me over the years in my struggle for sexual purity. I urge you too to hide these and other key Scriptures in your heart and mind.

Matthew 4:1-11 records the temptation of Jesus. When Satan tempted him the first time, Jesus quoted Scripture. Satan got the message and in the next temptation quoted Scripture himself. Jesus did not change his battle plan but just quoted another Scripture. Satan tempted our Lord a third time, and Jesus again quoted Scripture and commanded Satan to leave. If our sinless

Lord used Scripture to fight his battles with temptation, we need to do so even more. A believer neglecting to memorize Scripture in order to arm himself for the battle for sexual purity is like sending a ship to war with no missiles or a soldier into battle with no bullets. Such an error on our part is both foolish and deadly.

If you are serious about being sexually pure, you must get serious about Scripture memory. Any of us, even if we are living in purity, can be hit by impure thoughts or face an unexpected compromising situation and become aroused within seconds. Within several minutes our bodies can respond sexually. Anyone serious about purity must be able to recall Scripture *instantaneously*; there sometimes isn't time to talk to Christian brothers or look up a Bible passage. Due to the nature of the battle, we do not have the luxury of watching and praying during the calm before the storm or fumbling around in an unprepared state hoping to find the right weapons. We must be armed and ready, with a full load of torpedoes—spiritual truths from the Word of God, against which our enemy cannot stand.

KEY PRINCIPLE

To be pure in thought and behavior, we must hide the truths of God's Word in our hearts by memorizing key Scriptures and obeying them.

KEY VERSES

"How can a young man keep his way pure? By living according to your word. . . . I have hidden your word in my heart that I might not sin against you" (Psalm 119:9, 11).

DISCUSSION QUESTIONS

1. Have you taken the time to memorize Scripture verses to help you in your struggle? If so, which verses have proved most helpful? If you have not engaged in such memorization, why not? What have you found to be the biggest barrier to Bible memorization? The greatest benefit?

2. How many verses can you quote to a brother regarding purity? Do you find it easy or difficult to share in this way with fellow Christians? Why?

3. Think of one or two Christian men you know who are especially struggling in the area of sexual purity. Turn some of the Scriptures on purity into prayer to God on their behalf right now.

Face to Face,
Side by Side

In World War II the Germans sank hundreds of Allied vessels carrying supplies to Europe. The German subs operated in wolf packs, preying on ships in coordinated efforts to locate, isolate, and sink them. Their efforts almost succeeded in choking England and Russia. To counter this attack, ships were not allowed to go across the Atlantic or Arctic Oceans alone but rather had to travel in convoys. Warships would escort these convoys across the ocean, providing necessary firepower against wolf packs or air attacks. For further safety, the convoys would zigzag across the ocean, altering course and speed, particularly when in known enemy waters. Convoys successfully carried millions of tons of needed supplies for the war effort. The tactic was successful because of teamwork.

But sadly, on one occasion the Allies failed to follow the principle learned earlier in the war, causing a calamity in the Arctic Ocean. In June 1942 convoy PQ-17 left Iceland with thirty-six ships carrying much needed supplies from America to Murmansk, Russia. On the north side of the convoy were frozen ocean and icebergs. On the south side were German U-boats, the German air force, and the world's largest German battleship, the *Tirpitz*. The thirty-six ships of the convoy left port with a cargo valued at close to seven hundred million dollars—enough supplies to help the Russians keep from surrendering to the Nazis camped on the outskirts of Moscow. Due to various problems, three ships of the convoy had to return to port almost immediately, leaving thirty-three ships to make the voyage.

The convoy steamed slowly but steadily for another week, hiding under a thick fog bank before being detected by German reconnaissance planes. The convoy, escorted by both British and American warships, fended off wave after wave of German attack planes and German U-boats, these initial attacks sinking only one supply ship. With their combined firepower fairly formidable, the convoy and the warships worked together, stayed together in formation, and survived together.

Until intelligence reports stated that the *Tirpitz* was headed toward PQ-17. Officers decided to pull the escorting warships *away from the convoy* and move to a location where they could best encounter the great German battleship. The order was given for the remaining thirty-two ships to scatter and make their way independently over 300 miles, through enemy-controlled waters, to their port of delivery in Russia.

This occurred during the summer months in the Arctic, where literally the sun does not set. It was bright daylight twenty-four hours a day—no cover of darkness. Also, the Germans knew where the supply ships were heading, and those ships, without their escorts, were easy pickings for German U-boats and the Luftwaffe (air force). During the following several days, twenty-three ships were sunk. These ships carried more than 3,000 military vehicles, including 400 tanks, and 200 warplanes. Only a quarter of the 188,000 tons of cargo arrived in Russia. The Germans lost only five airplanes, and the great battleship *Tirpitz* never lifted anchor! The intelligence report was wrong!

The application for spiritual warfare is clear. We Christian men need each other. There is strength in numbers. When isolated and separated from our brothers, we are easy pickings for the enemy of our souls.

Another example from naval history graphically shows the danger of facing the enemy alone. On June 30, 1945, Japanese torpedoes struck the USS *Indianapolis* as she steamed unescorted across the South Pacific. Ironically, she had just successfully completed the delivery of the first atomic bomb scheduled to be dropped on Hiroshima. The *Indianapolis* had not been told that Japanese submarines had sunk another ship in the same general area just a week before. The first torpedo blew the bow off the ship. Seconds later a second torpedo stuck midships, immediately causing the loss of all electrical power. This prohibited the ship from sending out a distress signal. Twelve minutes later, at 12:18 A.M., the USS *Indianapolis* sank. Approximately 300 of the 1,200-man crew died at that time.

When the USS *Indianapolis* did not reach port at the appointed time, the ship was not even missed, due to the secrecy of her mission and poor accountability on the Navy's part. Therefore, no search planes were dispatched to look for her. Five days later a submarine patrol plane saw an oil slick in the water, went lower to investigate, and saw men from the *Indianapolis* floating in the water. Rescue planes were called in, but by the time the men were found and rescued, two thirds of the crew had been eaten by sharks.

If only there had been another friendly ship in the area, these men would not have died. If only the ship could have issued a distress signal asking for help. If only someone had missed them when they didn't show up on time at their home port. If only . . . Ecclesiastes 4:9-10, 12 says, "Two are better than one. . . . But pity the man who falls and has no one to help him up! . . . Though one may be overpowered, two can defend themselves. A cord of three strands is not quickly broken."

Second Timothy 2:22 urges us to "Flee the evil desires of youth, and pursue righteousness, faith, love and peace, *along with those who call on the Lord out of a pure heart*" (emphasis mine). The truth of this verse in regard to purity is twofold. First: "pursue." As believers, our lives have a purpose. The Scriptures lay out for us a clear direction to guide our steps and to run toward—living for and being like the Lord Jesus Christ. In Matthew 6:33 Jesus commands us to "Seek first his kingdom and his righteousness. . . ." Romans 13:14 says, "Clothe yourselves with the Lord Jesus Christ, and do not think about how to gratify the desires of the sinful nature." "Pursue righteousness [1 Corinthians 1:30 says, "Christ . . . is our righteousness"], faith [see Hebrews 11:6], love [see 1 Timothy 1:5] and peace [see Colossians 3:15], along with those who call on the Lord out of a pure heart."

The second thing we must do is to find those who are going in the direction we want to go, so we can walk there together. To again quote 2 Timothy 2:22, "along with those who call on the Lord out of a pure heart." Having buddies, fellow strugglers in the battle for purity, is indispensable. We need close companions, a team of confidants who will pray for us; who will listen compassionately and honestly when we confess our failings and stumblings; who will encourage us; who will rebuke us when appropriate; who know when we're traveling, where we're traveling, and whom we will see; whom we can run to when we're actually being tempted. Two examples come to mind.

The first example involves a friend I'll call Joe. Joe was an enlisted man in the military assigned to a relatively isolated base where prostitution and immoral living were the norm. Joe's only "Christian" buddy was fornicating with another "Christian" girl who was stationed at the same base. When Joe met a young woman on the base, their relationship progressed along physical lines, to a point where they too were sinning sexually. Joe confessed his struggles and failures to me and was grieved over the turn his life had taken. But he also commented that what made it hard for him to quit seeing this woman was that his only "Christian" male friend on the base was encouraging him in this immoral relationship. Joe needed to find a group of men who were seeking the Lord together and who were trying to live their lives in a pure way—"along with those who call on the Lord with a pure heart."

The other example involves another friend of mine. I'll call him Eric. Eric was struggling with impure thoughts and masturbation, though he wanted desperately to live a pure and holy life. Eric was involved in a Bible study group of other young men who also wanted to win the battle for sexual purity. In Matthew 5:8 Jesus promises, "Blessed are the pure in heart for they will see God," and he deeply desired such a spiritual state. Eric made a covenant with another brother who struggled in the same way that anytime he stumbled in this area, he would tell his brother. The other brother (I'll call him Tom) agreed to the mutual covenant. Almost every time Eric and Tom would get together, one would ask the other, "How are you doing in the area of purity?" Proverbs 27:17 says, "As iron sharpens iron, so one man sharpens another."

Their questioning of each other was a specific application of this verse to help each other in an area of mutual weakness.

As they both continued to stumble and fall in this area, they took another very challenging step. Eric and Tom agreed that if either one of them stumbled in this area of purity, if either of them yielded to the temptation to look at pornography or made provision for their flesh by masturbating, then both of them would spend the next day in prayer and fasting for each other.

Imagine that—two brothers who loved each other enough to commit to pray for each other and not to eat for twenty-four hours if either of them fell to temptation. This is an example of true brotherly love. When Eric felt tempted, he could call Tom, and Tom would pray for him. When Tom felt tempted, he would call Eric, and Eric would remind him how hungry he got the last time they both fasted. To return to Ecclesiastes 4, "Two are better than one, because they have a good return for their work: If one falls down, his friend can help him up. But pity the man who falls and has no one to help him up!" (verses 9-10). And look again at 2 Timothy 2:22: "Pursue righteousness, faith, love and peace, *along with those who call on the Lord out of a pure heart*" (emphasis mine).

What kind of friend or friends are you associating with? Are they friends who encourage you in your sin? Or maybe friends who are themselves caught in the web of sexual sin and are content to stay there? Or friends who see nothing wrong with sexual expression outside of marriage? Or do you have friends who call sexual sin for what it is—*sin*? Friends who will ask you the hard questions of accountability. Friends who will pray for you when you're tempted or will even fast with you during your trials and struggles. Committing to the pursuit of sexual purity may mean you have to leave your current "friends" because they are not really friends at all. Ask God to lead you to brothers whom you can trust and be honest with, who will share their struggles with you. James 4:2 says, "You do not have, because you do not ask God." And in Matthew 7:7 Jesus promises, "Ask and it will be given to you; seek and you will find; knock and the door will be opened to you." Keep asking the Lord until you find that special friend with whom you can share your heart. God never intended for us to fight this battle alone!

I wish I had really understood this as a young believer. One of the first verses I ever memorized was 1 Corinthians 10:13, "No temptation has seized you except what is common to man. And God is faithful; he will not let you be tempted beyond what you can bear. But when you are tempted, he will also provide a way out so that you can stand up under it." I used to think a lot about that verse, and I believed it in my head; but it wasn't working itself out in my life. I still fought desires to look at pornography and suffered from the consequent actions of masturbation and guilt that inevitably followed. Over and over again I'd find myself thinking thoughts that I knew were impure and sinful and thus unacceptable to God.

I was trapped by habits I had formed in my pre-puberty days. And now that I was a Christian, this verse, which was supposed to help and encourage me, actually became a stumbling block to me. The temptations I was facing were too strong for me to bear. My failures were so constant and oppressive that I came to believe 1 Corinthians 10:13 was simply not true. Despite what that verse said about "a way out," I was unable to say no to my temptations.

After struggling with this verse for some time, I concluded that since it was not true for me, since it wasn't working in my life, it must not be true—period. And if this verse wasn't true, maybe the whole Bible wasn't true. And if the Bible wasn't true, then there was no basis for believing in the existence of God. And if there really wasn't a God, there were no moral standards that made looking at pornography or masturbation wrong. So I indulged myself as much as I desired. It was quite easy actually. I had a position in the military that required me to inspect rooms for cleanliness, etc. In my inspections I would look not only for dirt and dust but also for pornography . . . and I could always find what I was looking for.

Every day I would look, lust, masturbate, and, to my surprise, feel guilty. If there really was no God, why was I experiencing guilt? I was perplexed about this. This continued for over a year. Not surprisingly, that was a year of spiritual darkness for me. Since I had concluded that God did not exist, I spent no time with Him in the Scriptures, I had no prayer life, and the fellowship I had enjoyed with close brothers became shallow because I was hiding my deepest struggles from them.

I know and understand now why I still had guilt feelings. Guilt is a real spiritual consequence when an offense against our holy God has been committed. My rationalizations had no effect on my conscience. The Holy Spirit who dwells in all believers did not accept my musings. The Righteous Judge spoke to me through my conscience to continually pronounce me "guilty, in need of repentance." How much better it is to have a clear conscience before God. First John 3:21 says, "Dear friends, if our hearts do not condemn us, we have confidence before God." May we, like the apostle Paul, "strive always to keep [our] conscience clear before God and man" (Acts 24:16).

In my foolish wisdom, I lived out the tragic situation portrayed in Ephesians 4:17-19:

So I tell you this, and insist on it in the Lord, that you must no longer live as the Gentiles do, in the futility of their thinking. They are darkened in their understanding and separated from the life of God because of the ignorance that is in them due to the hardening of their hearts. Having lost all sensitivity, they have given themselves over to sensuality so as to indulge in every kind of impurity, with a continual lust for more.

I felt separated from God and isolated from others. Because I didn't hear others speaking of their struggles for sexual purity, I concluded I was the only one in the world suffering from this form of temptation. Satan was surely reinforcing this wrong belief. Revelation 12:10 describes the enemy of our souls as "the accuser of our brothers, who accuses them before our God day and night." I felt too embarrassed to speak of this weakness and this sin in my life. I did not want to be rejected or thought of as a pervert. Rather, I wanted to be loved and accepted, to be esteemed. And the path I thought would take me there was to live a lie, to act as if I had no struggles, as if everything was OK in my life, as if I had no great need for prayer or healing. But of course the opposite was true. I had much in my life and soul that desperately needed deep change. And 1 Corinthians 10:13 was right: "No temptation has seized you except what is common to man."

I know now that this verse is true. Whenever I speak of my struggles with pornography and lust, many come forward to speak to me of their struggles, their trials, their failings, their weaknesses, their sinful habits. Oh, the comfort of this verse! I know that every sin I have ever committed, every sin I have contemplated or been tempted with, every other man has also been tempted with or done. On one hand it is discouraging that we as humans are so utterly sinful. But alone? Definitely not. A great company of people, believers and nonbelievers, struggle with sexual temptation. I'm not the only one. This doesn't excuse my sin, but it encourages me to know that others understand what I'm dealing with.

Friend, please don't fall prey to the enemy like I did. Memorize 1 Corinthians 10:13; believe it, rely on it, apply it to your life. Tell your closest buddy and/or pastor about your struggles. If you are in a fellowship group that is not honest enough with themselves, find a group that will be vulnerable and open and truthful with you. Every temptation you struggle with is common to others. You may feel alone, but you are not. Ask the Lord to lead you to someone in whom you can confide. He will be faithful, and "he will give you the desires of your heart" (Psalm 37:4).

KEY PRINCIPLE

Fellow strugglers working together and staying in close communication with God and each other can help one another stand strong in the battle for sexual purity.

KEY VERSES

"Two are better than one, because they have a good return for their work: If one falls down, his friend can help him up. But pity the man who falls and has no one to help him up! . . . Though one

may be overpowered, two can defend themselves. A cord of three strands is not quickly broken" (Ecclesiastes 4:9, 10, 12).

DISCUSSION QUESTIONS

1. Who do you know that understands your deepest struggles and temptations? Have you been able to discuss your battle with him candidly and compassionately? In a way that helps you maintain a holier walk with Christ? Why or why not?

2. Who do you know that has shared their struggles with you? Were you able to give caring, honest feedback? Why or why not? Was this an aid to the other person? In what way? How did helping him help you?

3. How can you find a brother to confide in and "convoy" with? What precautions do you need to observe as you seek such companions? What benefits do you anticipate as the convoy forms and begins to function? What steps can you take today, this week to bring this about?

CHAPTER
EIGHT

On Guard!

Bong! Bong! Bong! General Quarters, General Quarters! All hands man your battle stations. This is not a drill. I repeat, this is not a drill. Set Condition I steaming. Bong! Bong! Bong!" went the ship's alarm. Every man on our ship rushed to their battle stations. "General Quarters, General Quarters!"

My heart pounded within me. The captain came onto 1MC, the ship's announcing system: "Two Iranian fighter planes have been spotted on radar and are heading straight toward our battle group. We presume they are armed. We are attempting to warn them away from our position. If they activate their fire control radars, we will shoot them down."

It was 1979, and the Ayatollah Khomeini had seized American hostages from the American Embassy in Teheran, Iran. Just two weeks before the abductions, the USS *Bainbridge* had been steaming in the Indian Ocean on a routine seven-month, Western Pacific deployment. We were in Condition IV steaming, normal peacetime cruising. The ship was en route to Mombasa, Kenya, for a six-day port visit to be followed by exercises in the northern Arabian

Sea with the British, Pakistani, and U.S. navies. But as soon as the hostage situation developed, not wanting to antagonize the Iranians, both the British and Pakistani governments withdrew their Navies from the exercise. That left just the U.S. battle group, comprised of an aircraft carrier, the *Bainbridge*, and several other ships. After our Kenyan port visit, we steamed north to the Iranian coast and waited. Our task was to stand guard and do whatever the President and our military leaders asked to help recover the hostages and serve American interests.

The *Bainbridge* was a guided-missile-carrying, nuclear-powered cruiser. She had the latest air search radar in the Navy at that time. Since we didn't need constant refueling, we were the ship sent closest to Iran, fifteen to twenty miles away from the carrier. The first line of defense against attacking Iranian planes would be the carrier's own airplanes. Hopefully the battle would be an air battle 100 to 200 miles away from the carrier. The second line of defense, presuming the Iranians might try to sink the carrier, would be the screening ship's missiles. (Since we were the screening ship, we were the second line of defense.) If incoming Iranian planes got through the fighters and the ship's missiles, the third line of defense would be the carrier's own anti-air missiles.

Adrenaline pumped through every cell of my body. This was what we had trained for; this was what our ship was designed for. All the training, all the hours of practice, had prepared us for this moment. We were in Condition I steaming. All the watertight doors and hatches on the ship were shut and had been checked and rechecked to verify their closed position. Every man was in his assigned battle station. Every weapon was manned and armed for firing. Our ship put missiles on the rails of the launchers, ready to fire within seconds. All weapons systems were checked and rechecked. We all waited anxiously as the minutes ticked down, waiting for the Iranian jets to make their move. Damage control parties were dressed out, and lockers containing equipment to fight potential fires and stop anticipated flooding were being inventoried. We knew we might come under attack, and we were ready for whatever might happen.

The familiar cackle of the 1MC was heard. It was the Captain. "Secure from General Quarters, Secure from General Quarters. The Iranian jets turned back and are no longer a threat. Secure from General Quarters. Now set Condition II steaming."

On Navy ships different "Conditions of Readiness" are set depending on the possibility of war and danger to the ship. Condition I is General Quarters, all hands at their battle stations. This is the highest level of alert, the state of readiness from which a ship fights a war. Condition II steaming is a condition halfway between Condition I and Condition IV. Condition III is wartime cruising, with one third of the crew on watch and armaments manned in proportion to the threat. Condition IV is normal peacetime steaming. In this state, missiles and other armaments are not manned or made ready. The country is at peace; there is no expectation of attack from the air or submarines. As always on a ship at sea, a number of hatches and watertight doors are closed to prevent flooding in case of an accident, but there is no heightened state of war readiness. Condition V is peacetime watch in port. In this condition, normally about one third of the crew is away from the ship to visit their homes or whatever. One third of the crew is left on board the ship to handle any shipboard emergencies. The other third is on liberty. A ship is never left fully unguarded or unmanned.

In the battle for sexual purity, men also need to be aware of the conditions and cycles of their lives. As the threat to sexual purity increases, men must take appropriate precautions and actions to counter the threat. All ships have battle plans. Every sailor has an assigned post or position to man based on the Condition of Readiness required for the safety of the ship. In the same way, men need to have a thought-out sexual purity battle plan to meet the threat of temptation in their quest to keep pure. Men who struggle with purity must study themselves and their life situations to determine when they are most vulnerable. A plan of action must be prepared ahead of time to help them obey the Lord and keep pure.

Each man is different; the circumstances that cause one man to falter may not cause another to fall. One fellow I know stumbled every time there was a lot of stress in his life. Just prior to exams or major projects, he would find himself looking at pornography and acting out his lust. As he evaluated this pattern, he realized he was more susceptible at some times than at others. Another man struggled when he had a lot of idle, unscheduled time. Another guy knows that when he travels and is away from his wife and family, staying in hotel rooms, he is easily tempted. Another man I know struggles when he is alone in his own house. Luke 4 and Matthew 4 both record the temptation of Christ in the wilderness, but Luke 4:13 adds a dimension not found in the more familiar Matthew passage: "When the devil had finished all this tempting, he left him *until an opportune time*" (emphasis mine). Satan tempts us at the times he feels we will be least likely to be able to resist. He attacks us when we are least prepared, least ready, and most susceptible to a fall.

The story of David and Bathsheba offers another example of this. Second Samuel 11:1-5 says:

In the spring, at the time when kings go off to war, David sent Joab out with the king's men and the whole Israelite army. They destroyed the Ammonites and besieged Rabbah. But David remained in Jerusalem. One evening David got up from his bed and walked around on the roof of the palace. From the roof he saw a woman bathing. The woman was very beautiful, and David sent someone to find out about her. The man said, "Isn't this Bathsheba, the daughter of Eliam and the wife of Uriah the Hittite?" Then David sent messengers to get her. She came to him, and he slept with her. (She had purified herself from her uncleanness.) Then she went back home. The woman conceived and sent word to David, saying, "I am pregnant."

Why did David stay in Jerusalem, seeing that was "the time when kings go off to war"? Why was David sleeping in the afternoon and waking up at dusk? Where were David's other wives and concubines? David was not ready to face, let alone conquer, this temptation. At a time when kings go to war, he was not in the battle for sexual purity. What "an opportune time" for the enemy. Satan found a warrior who was supposed to be fighting, who was not with his troops, who was not doing what he was supposed to be doing. The king was isolated and idle. And David fell. He was a man after God's own heart, a godly man, mighty in the Spirit; but he fell. He was not a weak man, but he had a weak moment. For all men, that's all it takes for sexual sin to happen—a weak moment.

Since men are so quick to respond sexually, we must always be on our guard. There is an old expression that I learned when I first joined the Navy: "Eternal vigilance is the price for safety." We must be always watching, always alert, never letting our guard down. There are times when we know we are going to be tempted; there are times when we are relatively safe from temptation; there are times when enticement to evil stares us in the face unforeseen. We must learn to discern the times of our lives and prepare accordingly or we will fall.

After I left the Navy in 1982, I continued to minister to sailors assigned to the naval base in Alameda, California. The Navy has a policy that allows ships returning from a deployment to carry civilian friends and family members home with them. These non-Navy folks embark on the ship when it arrives in Hawaii and ride back to the mainland on the ship, normally about a six-day journey. I was asked by some sailor friends to go on one of these cruises. As I was spending time with the Lord prior to the trip, I was reading about the temptation of Christ in Matthew 4. The idea of fasting stood out to me. I was impressed that Jesus fasted for forty days prior to His temptation. I knew I would be tempted on the ship with pornography, and I felt the Lord telling me that I too should fast.

But I disobeyed the Spirit's prompting. Four days into the cruise, I walked into a berthing area where a number of sailors and other men were huddled around a TV and VCR, intently watching a movie. I walked over to see what they were cheering about. It was a pornographic movie. I had a split-second to decide what I was going to do. My choices were to obey the Lord and flee the area or stay and watch the porno flick. Literally hundreds of rationalizations flooded my mind. "I've never seen a movie like this—why not see this one?" "No one knows me, so it won't hurt my reputation." And so on. All the time that I was trying to decide whether or not I would obey the Lord, my eyes were watching the filth on the screen, and my flesh was liking what I was seeing.

I stayed and watched the movie, defiling myself and denying

my Lord. In my guilt and shame afterwards, I asked the Lord why I had not fled. He gracefully showed me that I had not adequately prepared myself for the coming threat. He knew that I would be faced with this temptation, and He had tried to prepare me, but I had disobeyed. I should have fasted and prayed in preparation for the cruise. I should have been more on guard during my time on board that ship. Because I failed to have a purity plan, I fell.

Prayer is essential for the victory of purity. In Daniel 10 we read that Daniel fasted and prayed for three weeks, after which he looked up and saw an angel from the Lord. Verses 12-14 tell us that the angel said:

> *"Do not be afraid, Daniel. Since the first day that you set your mind to gain understanding and to humble yourself before your God, your words were heard, and I have come in response to them. But the prince of the Persian kingdom resisted me twenty-one days. Then Michael, one of the chief princes, came to help me, because I was detained there with the king of Persia. Now I have come to explain to you what will happen to your people in the future, for the vision concerns a time yet to come."*

Daniel had prayed, and God sent an angel with the answer. But the answering angel was detained in spiritual warfare for twenty-one days until reinforcements came to help.

Because I chose not to fast and pray in preparation for the test I would face on that ship, I fell. Isaiah 32:8 says, "The noble man makes noble plans, and by noble deeds he stands." Part of being a wise or noble man is to live our lives by wise plans. The fellow I mentioned above who struggles with impurity when he is home alone developed the following purity battle plan:

1. He locked up the VCR and gave his wife the key.

2. He locked up the TV and gave his wife the combination to the lock on the TV cabinet.

3. He carried no money or credit cards. He knew that to rent impure videos takes money. So he carries no money with him.

4. He told several men and his wife about his struggles and asked them to hold him accountable. These accountability partners would regularly ask him questions about whether he was following his plan or not. They were also available to him for confession if he stumbled and prayer support if he was tempted.

I have heard that Billy Graham never travels alone; he always takes at least one man with him. Also, he will never be with or counsel another woman alone, other than his wife. He will also never get on an elevator alone. All these are part of his battle plan to live above reproach and to keep sexually pure. He has developed plans to avoid even an appearance of evil. The end result is a lifetime of faithful, faultless service to the Lord without a trace of sexual sin. Thank God for the Billy Grahams who provide such godly examples for us.

If Billy Graham can do it, God can give you and me the grace to be sexually pure also.

KEY PRINCIPLE

Each man must develop a sexual purity battle plan, recognizing the times and situations in which he is particularly vulnerable, then exercise that plan with vigilance and perseverance.

KEY VERSE

"The noble man makes noble plans, and by noble deeds he stands" (Isaiah 32:8).

DISCUSSION QUESTIONS

1. When are your vulnerable times? Does anyone else know about these? Why or why not? Why are you more susceptible during these times? What does that tell you about yourself?

2. Develop a plan to help you keep pure during your vulnerable times. What must this plan include to be workable for you? Aim high, but be realistic.

3. Share your plan with a friend who can and will hold you accountable. What criteria should this friend meet in order to be able to minister effectively to you in this way?

CHAPTER
NINE

Our Defeated
But Devious Foe

In early May 1982 two Argentine air force jets left their base at
Rio Grande, each carrying one Exocet missile (an air-to-sur-
face missile designed to sink ships). Their target? The British
Navy. The war was being fought between Britain and Argentina
for ownership of the Falkland Islands, located off the coast of
Argentina.

Flying fifty feet above the water and in strict radio and radar
silence, the two jets secretly approached the British fleet. When
they reached the target launch area, they fired the Exocets.
Neither pilot knew which ship the other had targeted. The jets
then turned around and headed back toward Argentina, undetected.

Once fired, Exocets stay at fifty feet or so above the surface
of the water for over twenty miles until they are only a mile or so
away from the designated target. Since the Exocet is much smaller
than the smallest airplane, a ship's radar may not even register its
presence on the screen, making it virtually undetectable.

The HMS *Sheffield* was steaming in waters just north of the

Falkland Islands. Exocet missiles were inbound, and the Argentine jets that had fired the missiles were already headed home. The only warning the HMS *Sheffield* had was one blip on the radar screen that immediately disappeared. The officers on the bridge saw a trail of smoke and the missile closing rapidly, but too late. The Exocets hit the ship at over 600 mph, carrying a payload of over 350 pounds. The force of the missile penetrated thirty feet into the ship. The HMS *Sheffield* had been hit by missiles, but the crew literally didn't know what hit them. The British vessel caught fire and sank four hours later.

Air attacks can be a one-time shot or can be sustained over a long period of time. In the recent Gulf War, the Coalition of countries trying to liberate Kuwait had air superiority during the entire war. For over 100 days, every day, the warplanes attacked Iraqi ground troops, tanks, missile sites, communications stations, etc. By the time the ground forces invaded Iraq and Kuwait, the Iraqi troops gladly and willingly gave up. Oppressive air warfare can do that in a war. In a spiritual sense, this nearly happened to me.

Several years ago I was under attack again. I reviewed the checklist in my mind regarding pornography. Were there emotional or psychological needs I was not taking to the Lord? Was I seeking to make pornography my refuge instead of God? Was I fearful, lonely, depressed, feeling like a failure, feeling rejected, or experiencing some other inner need? None of these things could be answered in the affirmative.

The attack was oppressive, and at first I didn't realize how all-encompassing it was. I found myself wanting to read the cheap, sensuous novels that are sold in food stores. I found myself desiring to slip into libraries to read the same types of novels—the kind that normally have a beautiful, half-naked girl on the front cover in the arms of some muscular, half-naked guy. I felt compelled to find one of these novels and read it in order to stir up lust. I didn't feel these urges when I was at home, but as soon as I stepped into my yard or left my house . . .

In almost any store I went into, be it a drugstore, food store, or video shop, I was sorely tempted. I was spending probably 80 percent of my available emotional energy fighting these temptations. I felt drained every day. I was afraid it was only a matter of time before I would "graduate" to some heinous sin. I also felt extremely guilty and vulnerable. I perpetually felt unclean and beyond God's forgiveness. I felt defeated and again started thinking that 1 Corinthians 10:13 was just not true: "No temptation has seized you except what is common to man. And God is faithful; he will not let you be tempted beyond what you can bear. But when you are tempted, he will also provide a way out so that you can stand up under it." "Baloney," I thought. "I *am* being tempted beyond my strength." I felt desperate, panicky.

This continued for almost six months. I was totally spent, ready to give up on everything related to the Christian life. I knew I couldn't go on this way. Every store was a stumbling block to me. The words of Proverbs 7:12 about the adulteress came to mind: "Now in the street, now in the squares, at every corner she lurks." I felt I could not go anywhere in any commercial district without being tempted. I cried out to the Lord for help, coming back to the One who was tempted in all ways like we were, but without sin, and who is able to help us. God answered by showing me a new insight about this battle for purity that has been tremendously helpful.

I was spending the weekend at a friend's house while I was at a conference, away from home. One day I scanned his bookshelf in the bedroom where I was staying, and one of the titles jumped out at me—*Destined to Overcome* by Paul Billheimer. I had read another one of his books and really liked it, so I picked this one up. I had been a believer for fifteen years but had never seen some of the truths Billheimer wrote about in that book.

The insight I received that day revolves around the question, how did Jesus' death defeat Satan? I knew that Scripture said Jesus won the victory for us, and I knew that Satan was truly defeated, but how? Think about Satan's involvement with three people in the Bible—Adam, Job, and Jesus. The ultimate goal of Satan in the Garden was to get Adam and Eve to sin by obeying his commands and so become subject to him. The methods he used to get to that point were to create doubt in Eve's mind regarding what God had said and to tempt her to eat the fruit. Satan, a liar, enticed Eve with a description of the wonderful things that would happen to her if she disobeyed and ate; namely, "your eyes will be opened, and you will be like God" (Genesis 3:5). We know that Adam and Eve ate the forbidden fruit. By that act they disobeyed God and willingly subjected themselves to Satan's authority. Now all of their offspring, all of us humans, inherit their sinful nature. Romans 5:12 says, "Therefore, just as sin entered the world through one man, and death through sin, and in this way death came to all men, because all sinned. . . ."

More of Satan's tactics of warfare are found in Job 1—2. Job was the most righteous man on earth. God even bragged about him to Satan. Satan's response was to say that Job's love and devotion to God were only for selfish reasons. "Let me take away his material possessions and his loved ones, and Job will curse you," the Devil boasted. God took up the challenge and granted Satan the freedom to afflict Job. We find the account in Job 1:13-22:

*One day when Job's sons and daughters were feasting and
drinking wine at the oldest brother's house, a messenger
came to Job and said, "The oxen were plowing and the
donkeys were grazing nearby, and the Sabeans attacked
and carried them off. They put the servants to the sword,
and I am the only one who has escaped to tell you!" While
he was still speaking, another messenger came and said,
"The fire of God fell from the sky and burned up the sheep
and the servants, and I am the only one who has escaped
to tell you!" While he was still speaking, another messenger came and said, "The Chaldeans formed three raiding
parties and swept down on your camels and carried them
off. They put the servants to the sword, and I am the only
one who has escaped to tell you!" While he was still speaking, yet another messenger came and said, "Your sons and
daughters were feasting and drinking wine at the oldest
brother's house, when suddenly a mighty wind swept in
from the desert and struck the four corners of the house. It
collapsed on them and they are dead, and I am the only one
who has escaped to tell you!" At this, Job got up and tore
his robe and shaved his head. Then he fell to the ground in
worship and said: "Naked I came from my mother's womb,
and naked I will depart. The LORD gave and the LORD has
taken away; may the name of the LORD be praised." In all*
this, Job did not sin by charging God with wrongdoing.
(emphasis mine)

In all this Satan did not get Job to sin. But Satan's motto is,
"If at first you don't succeed, try, try again." Satan's next tactic
was torture. Again there was an exchange of words between the
Lord and Satan, and again Satan was limited in that he could not
kill Job, though he could afflict him personally. And afflict him
he did. Job suffered horrible physical abuse, even having terrible
boils all over his body. Job suffered so intensely that he despaired

of life itself. He also suffered psychological affliction when most of his friends deserted him, and the ones who didn't leave him accused him falsely of some hidden sin. Job suffered even more abuse from the hands of his wife, who tried to get Job to "Curse God and die!" (2:9). The pattern that Satan used with Job was the same that he later tried on Jesus.

First Satan tried to kill baby Jesus outright. He stirred up jealousy in Herod so that the paranoid king had all of Bethlehem's baby boys two years old or younger put to death. Then Satan tried to tempt Jesus to sin in the wilderness, but again to no avail. I think Satan tried several other attempts on Jesus' life too, such as the sudden storm when Jesus and His disciples were caught in the middle of the lake. The disciples were convinced they were going to perish, while Jesus slept in the back of the boat. When the Savior awoke, He rebuked the winds and the waves, and they calmed down immediately. The same wind that killed Job's family was at work trying to kill Jesus, but it was not yet Jesus' time.

During Jesus ministry, He also incurred psychological suffering, being constantly misunderstood and finally abandoned by his friends in his hour of need. He was left alone to be abused by the religious leaders, who conducted improper and illegal trials against Him. But in all this, Jesus did not sin.

I think at this point Satan gambled. We know that from the beginning of time Satan did not fully understand God's plan. I think Satan figured he could physically torture Jesus so much through the Roman crucifixion process that Jesus would sin somewhere along the way. Jesus was given thirty-nine strokes with the whip. His beard was plucked out. He was deprived of food and water and sleep during His trials. Weak, beaten, suffering from loss of blood, stripped naked, He was hung on a cross to die. Jesus had thousands of angels at his disposal whom He could have called upon to deliver Him from the torture. He could have used His powers of Deity to open up the earth like an earthquake to swallow up His accusers. He could have done a myriad of things, but His love for us kept Him on the cross. He had power to lay down His life and power to take it up again; He did not *have* to endure what He endured—it could happen only by His choice. In all this Jesus did not sin. Satan's gamble completely failed.

Since the beginning of time, every victim of death had sinned and so deserved to die, thus putting themselves under the control of the Devil. But Satan really overstepped his bounds when he empowered evil men to kill an innocent, sinless son of Adam, who was actually also the Son of God. (In another sense, Satan did not kill Jesus, nor did wicked men. Jesus said, "I lay down my life—only to take it up again. No one takes it from me, but I lay it down of my own accord. I have authority to lay it down and authority to take it up again," John 10:17-18.) Now for the first time a man, a descendant of Adam, had not sinned and yet died. However, not only did Jesus die, but He rose again from the dead, proving once and for all that sin, death, and the Devil have no power over Him. And not only is this true for Him, but for all who believe in Jesus. We are united with Him in His death and in His resurrection (a study of Romans 6, especially verses 4-5, 8-11, 13, is helpful on this point).

Thanks to the atoning work of Jesus Christ, we have been set free from the Devil and from death and sin. Hebrews 2:14-15 says, "Since the children have flesh and blood, he too shared in their humanity so that by his death he might destroy him who holds the power of death—that is, the devil—and free those who all their lives were held in slavery by their fear of death."

As believers, because of our union with Christ, we have power over the evil one and his fellow demons. Matthew 18:18 tells us that Jesus promised, "I tell you the truth, whatever you bind on earth will be bound in heaven, and whatever you loose on earth will be loosed in heaven." The blood of Jesus is powerful!

When I came to understand these truths, I became aware that my sense of oppression because of a constant craving to lust over pornography might have a demonic connection. Maybe I was being regularly hit by missiles fired from demons of lust. I then prayed something like, "Lord Jesus, thank You for dying for me and for Your death, burial, and resurrection on my behalf. I acknowledge again Your lordship over me and rejoice that I am part of Your family because of Your finished work on the cross. In Your name, Lord Jesus, I renounce all sinful activities connected with pornography and lust in my life. By the power of Your name and Your blood, I command any and all demons of lust, pornography, impure thoughts, and immorality to leave me and to go where You send them. Thank You, Lord, for Your mighty power and for the authority You have given me as one of Your children."

Upon offering that prayer, I felt an immediate release, even a physical lifting of weight off my shoulders. The oppression and darkness I had carried immediately disappeared. I felt a freedom that I hadn't known for months. I was jubilant. Praise God for the liberty only He can give us!

I started wondering how long I had been under such demonic influence in my life. I wondered how many times I had been demonically guided toward pornography and found myself lacking energy to resist, thus yielding to temptation. I was responsible for my actions, but the enemy had certainly lured me into failure. I could think back to literally hundreds of instances where I was confronted with pornography without having consciously looked for it. Perhaps many times I had been set up for failure through Satan's manipulation of the world's system and so-called chance encounters.

Think back again to the illustration of a surface warfare ship. For years I had fought the battle for sexual purity on one level only, but that wasn't enough. A warship has to be able to sink other ships but must also be able to defend itself from threats in the air. It would be stupid to fire ship-to-ship missiles or torpe-does at an attacking airplane. Yet spiritually this is exactly what I had been doing for years. I did not even know I was being attacked from the air, by Satan and his demons. Ephesians 2:1-3 says:

> *You were dead in your transgressions and sins, in which you used to live when you followed the ways of this world and of* the ruler of the kingdom of the air, *the spirit who is now at work in those who are disobedient. All of us also lived among them at one time, gratifying the cravings of our sinful nature and following its desires and thoughts. Like the rest, we were by nature objects of wrath. (emphasis mine)*

From a spiritual warfare perspective, the air threat includes all demonic or satanic influence that tempts us to sin. The method God gave us for victory is not to run from the battle, but to *resist* evil spirits. James 4:7-8 says, "Submit yourselves, then, to God. Resist the devil, and he will flee from you. Come near to God and he will come near to you." We must offer spiritual resistance just as Jesus did when He was tempted. Our Lord used memorized Scripture to counter the claims, suggestions, and lies of the

enemy, and we must do the same. When we sense ourselves thinking or feeling something contrary to God, we must follow the
admonition of 2 Corinthians 10:5—"we take captive every
thought to make it obedient to Christ." That is the standard of
holiness God wants for us—every thought surrendered to Him.
"Resist the devil, and he will flee from you." This is a fantastic
promise from God that we must actively claim. We should cry out
as Jesus did, "Away from me, Satan!" (Matthew 4:10), then
immerse ourselves in God's Word as Jesus did, drawing near to
Him through prayer.

I asked this before, but I want to ask it again: Have you ever
been praying when suddenly your mind was filled with garbage?
Or have you ever been reading or studying the Bible when for no
explainable reason you saw in your mind a sensuous scene from
a movie or a sinful life experience you had tried to forget? It's
almost as if some demon, in cooperation with our fleshly mind,
pushes the Play button on the VCR of our brains and yells out
"Remember this?" If this has happened to you, you have been
assaulted with an enemy missile. Just as the HMS *Sheffield* was
hit by Exocet missiles and didn't know what hit her, you have
been bombarded with lustful suggestions by the enemy of our
souls.

When the missile hits and the thought is planted in our
brain, what should we do? We have to choose whether we will
entertain those thoughts or resist them and think of something
else. We must quickly cry out to God and pray the truths of
Romans 6. "Resist the devil, and he will flee from you" is not
wishful thinking but a promise from God, and not only a
promise but a weapon we must employ in our battle for purity.
Ephesians 6:11-18 says:

*Put on the full armor of God so that you can take your stand
against the devil's schemes. For our struggle is not against
flesh and blood, but against the rulers, against the authori-
ties, against the powers of this dark world and against the
spiritual forces of evil in the heavenly realms. Therefore put
on the full armor of God, so that when the day of evil comes,
you may be able to stand your ground, and after you have
done everything, to stand. Stand firm then, with the belt of
truth buckled around your waist, with the breastplate of righteousness in place, and with your feet fitted with the readiness that comes from the gospel of peace. In addition to all
this, take up the shield of faith, with which you can extinguish
all the flaming arrows of the evil one. Take the helmet of salvation and the sword of the Spirit, which is the word of God.
And pray in the Spirit on all occasions with all kinds of
prayers and requests. With this in mind, be alert and always
keep on praying for all the saints.*

When we resist the Devil in this way, we are utilizing the
weapons of warfare the Lord has so graciously given to us. Use
the sword of the Spirit boldly and skillfully. Pray with the authority of a child of the King. God promises us, "Resist the devil, and
he will flee from you." Believe it!

KEY PRINCIPLE

*Only as we submit to God and resist the Devil, relying on Christ,
not ourselves, to make us victorious, will we be sexually pure.*

KEY VERSES

*"Submit yourselves, then, to God. Resist the devil, and he will flee
from you. Come near to God and he will come near to you. Wash*

your hands, you sinners, and purify your hearts, you double-minded" (James 4:7-8).

DISCUSSION QUESTIONS

1. Do you believe there are demons of lust, immorality, etc? How have they impacted your life overall, in your home, at your work, in your church, in your community?

2. Have you ever experienced the type of unprovoked attacks of lust the author describes? How did you react? How do you wish you had reacted?

3. What have you done to resist the Devil in the past? Was this successful or unsuccessful? Why? What do you need to do to experience greater or more consistent victory in your battle for sexual purity?

When Past Hurts
Make Us Hide

The chief threat to a Navy surface ship is that of the submarine, designed to operate quietly and stealthily. In addition to those physical advantages, the submarine has an ally in the ocean itself—not just the ocean's depth but its temperature. As the ocean gets deeper, temperature drops; a rapid temperature drop over a short depth change is called a thermal layer. A surface ship will bounce sound waves (sonar) off the submarine to locate it. However, if the sound waves hit a thermal layer, they bounce back. Since the surface ship's sonar can't penetrate the thermal layer, the submarine continues to operate undetected.

There are several ways to penetrate such a layer. A ship or helicopter can lower a portable sonar device into the water until the sonar device is below the thermal layer. The sound waves can then pick up the image of a submarine if one is present. Or a friendly submarine can operate in the same area and at the same operating depth as the enemy submarine and use its sonar to detect the enemy. Either way, naval forces must have the ability to get below the thermal layer with sonar in order to detect the presence of the enemy and protect the surface ship. Failure to do so could result in the sinking of the ship, and the ship would not even know where the attack came from.

A submarine hiding under a thermal layer in the ocean illustrates many men who hide their true feelings, deep hurts, and past pains under a mask of self-sufficiency (which our culture mistakenly calls true masculinity) or false notions of true spirituality. In our society, for a man to display an emotion other than anger is considered a sign of weakness; for men to express emotional pain or hurt is unmasculine. Men verbalizing their needs goes against the grain of individualism and self-sufficiency. Young boys are trained to be emotional rocks, and as Simon and Garfunkel say in one of their songs, "A rock feels no pain." Real men don't cry, or so we are told.

But men are human beings created in the image of the true God, who has emotions—joy, anger, sadness. God designed all humans to have emotions, to be able to make decisions, to think rational thoughts, and to know internally through our consciences the rightness or wrongness of our actions and motives. Suppressed emotions always find a way of expressing themselves. The pains and hurts of the past can be dealt with in a godly way—through the blood of Christ, or they can be ignored and attempts made to deaden or escape from them.

Some men turn to booze to escape. Others turn to eating, others to gambling. Some get hooked on drugs, others on the adrenaline rush that comes from driving fast cars. Many turn to sex or pornography. For some, it doesn't even matter if the sexual outlet is male or female. For many men sexual orgasm provides an escape from pain and the hurts of the past. These same men may deny any connection at all between their past wounds and their current behavior (and obviously our present struggles can't be explained solely in terms of past crises or difficulties, though they also can't be explained apart from them). These men have constructed an emotional layer as impenetrable as the thermal layer of the ocean that hides a submarine.

I have been meeting and discipling men for nearly twenty-five years. Men I have met with personally who struggle with sexual sin had constructed an emotional layer of protection insulating them from past hurts. For many of these men the divorce of their parents caused grievous harm. Others had an emotionally distant or physically absent father. Others experienced significant failure in their lives—maybe their own divorce or failed athletic accomplishment. In the course of trying to cope with their pain, these men found sexual release to be a pain softener. The subsequent guilt is acceptable for many because it hurts less than the previous pain. Again, present behavior cannot be fully explained or blamed on past hurts, but those hurts are nevertheless a significant factor.

THE CONSTRUCTION
OF MY THERMAL LAYER

In my own life, even after walking with the Lord for over fifteen years I still battled the desire to look at pornography. I couldn't figure out why pornography was so attractive to me. I sought help from a man trained in pastoral counseling, and he became the sonar that dipped below my protective layer to locate the pain I was hiding from. He took me back to when my parents divorced and asked me to reconstruct everything I could remember. I have found that many of the elements in my life and struggles also reside in the lives of the men whom I counsel and disciple.

When I was about ten years old and approaching puberty, my father abandoned our family without warning. The night he left, my mother clung to him and kept crying out, "Don't leave me, please don't leave me." My brother and three sisters were in various states of emotional turmoil. We were all scared and crying and tried to convince my dad to stay. Both parents yelled at us to go back to our rooms, but we didn't want to. I had never seen my mother cry like that; in fact, I couldn't recall ever seeing her cry before.

When my dad finally left with some of his possessions, our household settled down in stunned silence, broken only by occasional sobs and outbursts of tears. I was stunned. Where did he go? Why did he leave me? What had I done to cause this? I felt afraid, abandoned, rejected, and unloved. I would have stopped him or gone with him if I could have, but he wouldn't let me. I was also angry with him for what he was doing to our family. I felt naked, like a piece of me was missing. I don't remember this, but my oldest sister says I cried nonstop for three days. Then I just shriveled up inside.

In our neighborhood a bunch of boys close to my age were going through the same things I was. So we formed a "gang." Several of us had tents in our backyards where we would meet. One of the boys would sneak his father's magazines out to us, and we would laugh at the pictures. The older boys taught me how to act out my lust before I even reached puberty. We would spend hours lusting after these pictures, fantasizing what sex would be like. I wanted to be loved and accepted, and that group of boys became my only source of affection and acceptance. Sex was not the only thing we did together, but it occupied a major part of our time.

I didn't realize it at the time, but I was actually developing many unhealthy physical, mental, and emotional patterns. I was also developing my thermal layer. Whenever I felt any of the core emotional feelings I'd felt the night my dad abandoned us, I would run to pornography. If I felt rejected, I'd want to look at more pornography—the girls in the magazines never look like they're rejecting you. If I felt guilty or alone or afraid, I would run to find comfort in pornography. If I felt out of control or unmanly, I would use pornography to fantasize how manly and in control I was. Even after becoming a Christian, even after becoming a missionary, I struggled with pornography. I just didn't know why.

In the years following my parents' divorce, I became numb and convinced myself that the divorce had no effect on me. I denied the hurt and the pain I had so deeply felt. Anytime someone offered to help me look at my past, I rejected their concern. I was trapped by the lure and lies of pornography, trapped by the pain of my past, trapped by a culture that told me that any display of emotion was a sign of weakness. I was denying my own humanity.

Anytime I felt fear, anger, unmanliness, loss of control, anxiety, rejection, etc, my hidden emotions would prompt me to look for pornography. I would slip into the cycle of temptation, find pornography, lust and fantasize, masturbate, feel guilty, repent, resolve not to look again. But I would soon feel one of the aforementioned emotions and find myself stumbling once more. I spent a lot of time in this deadly cycle.

A THERMAL LAYER EXPOSED

An understanding of the emotional layer in my life came via a man trained in pastoral counseling who works for the same missions group I work for. I asked Dick Stiliha why I could not cry and why I had a continuing hunger for pornography. Through his counseling, God allowed me to see the emotional deadening I had experienced.

Pornography had become my refuge. Worse, pornography was an idol for me, and I was its slave. I had things backwards in my life. *God* wants to be my refuge. When I hurt, God wants me to come to Him for comfort. When I feel rejected, He wants me to talk to Him about it. When I am worried or afraid, He wants me to cast my anxieties upon Him. When I feel lonely, He wants me to realize He is with me all the time. Psalm 62:8 says, "Trust in him at all times, O people; pour out your hearts to him, for God is our refuge." I had accepted a perverse idolatry. I had substituted pornography in the place of God!

Romans 1:21-26 speaks to this very thing:

For although they knew God, they neither glorified him as God nor gave thanks to him, but their thinking became futile and their foolish hearts were darkened. Although they claimed to be wise, they became fools and exchanged the glory of the immortal God for images made to look like mortal man and birds and animals and reptiles. Therefore God gave them over in the sinful desires of their hearts to sexual impurity for the degrading of their bodies with one another. They exchanged the truth of God for a lie, and worshiped and served created things rather than the Creator—who is forever praised. Amen. Because of this, God gave them over to shameful lusts.

In my struggles with pornography, I have observed that my failure to exercise self-control is directly related to my neglecting to worship God. If my desire to worship God, my Creator, is low, my desire for sexual impurity is high. And when I seek to glorify God and give thanks to Him, my desire for pornography is low to non-existent.

In their book *The Blessing*, John Trent and Gary Smalley write about parents' blessing their children. The authors describe seven adult personality types that result when a child grows up without "the blessing" of their parents. One of those types described me almost exactly—"the driven." "The driven" perform or produce in hopes of being accepted. It's hard for a driven person to say no because he fears rejection. Driven people work long hours, take on more projects than they can possibly do well, yet continue working harder and harder and longer and longer. Their worth is wrapped up in what they accomplish. Whether they are seeking additional educational degrees or higher wages or another promotion, the goal is the same—acceptance.

As I read *The Blessing*, I thought again of 2 Corinthians 10:3-5, and God showed me another "stronghold" in my life that He wanted to take down. That passage says, "For though we live in the world, we do not wage war as the world does. The weapons we fight with are not the weapons of the world. On the contrary, they have divine power *to demolish strongholds*. We demolish arguments and every pretension that sets itself up against the knowledge of God, and we take captive every thought to make it obedient to Christ." The "stronghold" in my life involved my motivation for many of my actions: to gain acceptance by others or to justify my existence. Subconsciously I felt that unless I achieved a certain position or rank or recognizable accomplishment, I had no intrinsic worth as a person. My work became my identity. If I spoke or taught a class and I got negative feedback, I felt rejected. If I worked my hardest but was criticized because it wasn't perfect, again I felt rejected. The end result was ever a feeling of being rejected or unloved.

My view of God also required repair. A child's relationship with his earthly father serves as a model for his relationship with God. If a man views his earthy father as domineering, he will view God in the same way. If a man's earthly father has an explosive temper, he will view God as having an explosive temper. Looking back, because I felt that my dad's acceptance of me was based solely on my performance, that was how I approached God. In order for God to love me, I had to do something for Him—lead someone to Christ, memorize another verse, have a consistent devotional time, do in-depth Bible study, etc. My Christian life mirrored my life in my family. I had learned from my parents that to be accepted, I had to perform; therefore, to be loved and accepted by God, I had to perform for Him.

The psychological patterns I had developed (unhealthy or confused responses to inner emotional hurts) led me to the habitual consumption of pornography. Since I felt rejected most of the time because my efforts weren't perfect or my performance wasn't acceptable, I'd run to pornography to hide the pain of perceived or actual rejection. In pornography, the girls are always looking at the camera in a way that communicates acceptance, the very thing I was seeking. I was trapped. In my head I could acknowledge the unconditional love of Christ taught in the Bible, but I could not grasp it in my heart.

Yet the Scriptures teach this love of God repeatedly. The question comes down to this: who am I going to believe—my feelings of worthlessness and of being unloved, or what God's Word says about me? God says He loves me, but I don't feel loved. Do my feelings negate God's Word? As the apostle Paul would say, "By no means!" Similarly, 1 John 1:9 says, "If we confess our sins, he is faithful and just and will forgive us our sins and purify us from all unrighteousness." Many times I don't feel clean after confessing my sins to God. But I know that my feelings regarding confession are just that—feelings. I have learned to step out in faith and believe 1 John 1:9, and I must do the same with the other promises of God.

Knowing these things should provide a safeguard for me against the temptation to indulge in pornography or commit any other sexual sin. I must keep before me the truth that my value as a person does not depend on the quality of what I am doing or the end result of my efforts. I am supposed to do my best, relying on God to help me, and to work for the glory of God. But if things don't turn out as expected, that doesn't mean God will stop loving me or will reject me.

The curious thing about this "stronghold" is that my performance and achievements made me look very secure and projected an appearance of healthy self-esteem. But it was all a mask hiding my fear of inadequacy. Larry Crabb speaks about this in his book *Encouragement*. What I just described about myself is seen in what Adam did in the Garden of Eden. After Adam sinned, he hid from God. When God approached him in the Garden, Adam exclaimed, "I was afraid because I was naked; so I hid" (Genesis 3:10). That became the pattern of my life. I felt naked because I knew my own sinfulness and weakness. I felt unworthy and unlovable. I felt afraid because I knew that if anyone really looked at me, they would see all my flaws, and I feared they would then reject me. So I "hid" behind the fig leaves of achievement and status. But, sadly, I still felt alone.

What about you? If you struggle with sexual sin, look deeper

into your life—your motives and your fears. Ask God to open
your eyes and to allow you to see yourself as God sees you. Study
God's love and unconditional acceptance of you. Believe God's
promises. Don't allow the flesh to deaden you in your pain; don't
hide behind a slick, lying approach to life—the lie of pornography. If you were in the room with that model in the magazine, do
you think she would look at you the same way? Do you think that
you could really have sex with that person without any consequences? Pornography never shows you its victims—the sexually
transmitted diseases, the emotional scars and damage, the rapes,
murders, and broken families. Pornography, like its author, the
enemy of our souls, misrepresents and distorts and destroys.

If you are struggling with pornography or some other sexual
sin, ask God to reveal any emotional layers under which you are
hiding. Ask Him to show you any repressed hurts. If you suspect
such things are there, ask God to lead you to a trusted friend, pastor, or counselor to help you get beneath the layer you have constructed.

Our God is a jealous God. Ask Him to show you if you have
made the pursuit of sexual pleasure an idol. God accepts no rivals;
He desires your total and complete devotion. Are you running
away from God and seeking fulfillment through sexual sin in
order to deaden the real hurts in your life? Your life can change
direction only with God's help.

When you are feeling the pull to look at pornography or the
desire to sin sexually, evaluate your life of worship. Go back to
Romans 6 and reckon yourself dead to sin. Memorize Psalm 62:8
or other key Bible texts. Ask God to heal you and to allow you to
understand hidden emotions that may be driving you to want to sin.
Make time to pour out your heart to God, who is your refuge. Spend

time reading the Psalms. David was a man after God's own heart; but he was full of emotion, and he expressed that emotion to God in his writings. He prayed for vengeance on his enemies, expressed anger to God, and let his heart sing with joy. Ask God to help you be a healthy man—in touch with your emotions, yet handling those emotions in a godly way, giving them to the Refuge of our souls.

A TORPEDO SHOT

Like the apostle Paul, I can say, "Not that I have already obtained . . . or have already been made perfect, but I press on . . ." (Philippians 3:12). I still find myself sometimes tempted to seek out pornography and thus escape emotional pain. I think of one time in my life in particular when I was struggling in this way. I asked God to give me understanding about myself, to show me what I was seeking to gain. The Holy Spirit brought James 3 to my mind:

> *Who is wise and understanding among you? Let him show it by his good life, by deeds done in the humility that comes from wisdom. But if you harbor bitter envy and selfish ambition in your hearts, do not boast about it or deny the truth. Such "wisdom" does not come down from heaven but is earthly, unspiritual, of the devil. For* where you have envy and selfish ambition, there you find disorder and every evil practice. *But the wisdom that comes from heaven is first of all pure; then peace-loving, considerate, submissive, full of mercy and good fruit, impartial and sincere. Peacemakers who sow in peace raise a harvest of righteousness.*
> *—Verses 13-18 (emphasis mine)*

The Holy Spirit was showing me what prompted me to want to look at pornography—"envy and selfish ambition." God could

see right through me; He understood me perfectly. I had recently
attended a meeting about three hours from my house. Attending
that meeting were men who were on the leadership team of the
Christian organization with which I minister. At one point in time
I'd felt I should have been made part of that team ("envy"). I had
also felt I had to constantly lobby for selection to the leadership
team ("selfish ambition"). As the Holy Spirit showed me the root
cause of my longings, I felt humbled and exposed. I also felt my
desire to look at pornography melting away. It was like surgically
removing the fangs from a snake. You don't fear the snake any-
more once you know it can't hurt you.

As I thought back on my involvement with leaders or those
in position over me organizationally, I discerned a similar pattern.
Before the meetings I felt fear—fear that I wouldn't be liked or
accepted, fear that I would say or do something not spiritually or
politically correct, fear that I wouldn't be perceived as warm or
loving or as having what it takes to be a leader. At the meetings I
would have many of the same fears. I continually felt the need to
fight for issues that were important to me and to risk confronta-
tion with the leaders regarding those issues. Afterwards I would
regret that I had even opened my mouth. After the meetings, one
of my brothers on the team would tell me how I had done, whom
I had offended, how I should have said things differently, etc. This
tortuous cycle always revolved around leadership or a position of
authority.

How true God's Word is! "Where you have envy and selfish
ambition, there you find disorder and every evil practice." The act
of looking at pornography is a vile practice, a dangerous diversion
away from dealing with real issues.

The core issue was the sovereignty of God: did I trust the God of infinite wisdom and love to place me where He desires? The issue of personal significance is not based on a title or position, but on who I am in Christ and what He thinks about me. If we rightly understand that, all else will fall into place, and we will be happy and productive as we walk with Jesus day by day.

KEY PRINCIPLE

Hiding beneath past wounds and present emotional pain makes us vulnerable to sexual impurity; but as we take refuge in God, we can win the battle.

KEY VERSE

"Trust in him at all times, O people; pour out your hearts to him, for God is our refuge" (Psalm 62:8).

DISCUSSION QUESTIONS

1. What protective layers do you tend to hide behind—emotional, spiritual, or whatever? Can you remember the circumstances during which these layers came into being? Looking back, would you have handled the situation differently? In what way?

2. Do you feel it is really possible for a man to hide under such layers and even to deny their existence? How do you feel about accepting God's help in taking your layers down? Do you feel comforted or threatened at such a prospect? Why?

3. Which tactics might work and which might not as you try to help a friend see his layers? Why? Could sharing your own

experiences at identifying and moving beyond your layers be helpful to your friend? In what way?

4. What idols do you run to for refuge? Why do you hurry there rather than to God? What generally is the result of this activity? Are you content with the results? Why or why not? If not, what should you do instead (be as specific as possible)?

CHAPTER
ELEVEN

A Call to Self-Discipline

One of the hardest things about the Christian life is to keep balanced. The Scriptures teach that we are destined to be "holy and blameless in his sight" (Ephesians 1:4), but they also tell us to "make every effort . . . to be holy; without holiness no one will see the Lord" (Hebrews 12:14). We *are* holy, and yet we are to *pursue* holiness. We know that God loves us and accepts us unconditionally. What I do will not cause His love for me to grow or make it diminish. My fellowship with Him can be temporarily broken, and I can use His mercy as a license for the flesh, but His love for me is a constant. And because He loves me, He expects me to grow in grace and in my commitment to and disciplined service for Him.

I once listened to a radio preacher who had a deliverance ministry. He said that a lot of people were coming to him for deliverance though they had already been delivered. All they needed to do was to take responsibility for themselves and to start exercising their wills, relying on Christ, in order to discipline their flesh. No one was in the car with me at the time, so I yelled "Amen" back to the preacher. As I thought about that brother's comments, some verses I'd memorized started coming to mind.

Psalm 50:16-17 says, "But to the wicked, God says: 'What right have you to recite my laws or take my covenant on your lips? You hate my instruction and cast my words behind you.'" Later he says in verse 23, "He who sacrifices thank offerings honors me, and he prepares the way so that I may show him the salvation of God." Second Timothy 2:20-22 adds: "In a large house there are articles not only of gold and silver, but also of wood and clay; some are for noble purposes and some for ignoble. If a man cleanses himself from the latter, he will be an instrument for noble purposes, made holy, useful to the Master and prepared to do any good work. Flee the evil desires of youth, and pursue righteousness, faith, love and peace, along with those who call on the Lord out of a pure heart."

These passage make clear *my* responsibilities. I have a free will, and I have the ability to make choices about what I will or will not do. Yes, I have developed sinful patterns in my life, but I have a responsibility now as a believer in Christ to change those patterns. Because of pains from my past, I developed defensive strategies to cope and to survive. But now that the Lord has revealed some of these to me and has shown me what He wants me to do about them, I have a responsibility through His power to repent and to change and to develop new ways of dealing with those hurts. Yes, I have been influenced by demonic deceptions and enticements, but now, through the Lord's grace, I know how to respond to those I'm able to recognize. I must choose again and again whether I will respond with sin or with obedience to Christ.

I recently completed a two-day fast. I had decided that if I looked at pornography, I would discipline myself by not eating for two days. I am not doing this to spank or mutilate myself. I am mindful of Colossians 2:20-23:

> *Since you died with Christ to the basic principles of this world, why, as though you still belonged to it, do you submit to its rules: "Do not handle! Do not taste! Do not touch!"? These are all destined to perish with use, because they are based on human commands and teachings. Such regulations indeed have an appearance of wisdom, with their self-imposed worship, their false humility and their harsh treatment of the body, but they lack any value in restraining sensual indulgence.*

I know that fasting in itself will not help me in "restraining sensual indulgence." Then why fast? When I choose to look at pornography, my mind has harbored fleshly thoughts that I then act out. When I want to look at pornography, my time of personal worship of the living God has not been from the heart. I have been walking in the flesh and not in the Spirit. I have not been reading, studying, and meditating on the Holy Scriptures. I am susceptible to the lures of pornography because I have concerns, fears, or other deep emotions that I am out of touch with and need to bring to my heavenly Father.

Fasting helps me center my whole being on Jesus Christ, "so that in everything he might have the supremacy" (Colossians 1:18). It helps me focus on God in prayer and get my mind off the flesh. Deliberately saying no to my desires for food helps me discipline my body and say no to its other desires (compare 1 Corinthians 9:27). This helps me check the direction of my life and make sure I am pursuing God. Physically, fasting cleanses our bodies; combined with the Word, it also can cleanse our spirits, souls, and minds.

Looking at pornography is like falling into a tar pit. It stains us, traps us, and sucks us in deeper. The images become etched in our memory and can be a source of stumbling as long as we live. James 1:27 says, "Religion that God our Father accepts as pure and faultless is this . . . to keep oneself from being polluted by the world." Pornography pollutes and tarnishes the one who looks at it.

For me, fasting is a God-given way of cleansing or purifying myself from what is "ignoble" in order to restore my service to the Lord. It is not an attempt to get God to love me more or to earn my way back into friendship with Him. I am forgiven as soon as I confess my sin. Rather, fasting is an attempt to again obey the Scriptures after I have broken them. I am not talking about putting myself under the Law, and this has nothing to do with salvation or works done to merit God's favor. It is only by grace that I or anyone else is saved. To me, the reason for fasting (and other acts of obedience to God) is expressed in Philippians 2:12-13, "Therefore, my dear friends, as you have always obeyed—not only in my presence, but now much more in my absence—continue to work out your salvation with fear and trembling, for it is God who works in you to will and to act according to his good purpose." Fasting is one way to "work out [my] salvation"—that is, to allow what God has done in my heart to work itself out, to show itself, throughout my life.

Other men may discipline themselves in different ways. I know men who struggle with purity who will not watch *any* movies. Others I know will not watch any "R" rated movies, and some draw the line down to "PG" or "PG-13." Another man, mentioned earlier in this book, struggles with even having a VCR in his home. He locked it up and gave his wife the key. We must make our own choices in these areas, but the important thing is that we develop a God-centered self-discipline.

I do other things to discipline myself as well. Since bookstores have been a stumbling block for me, I do not go into them unless my wife is with me. In grocery stores, I avoid the magazine aisle if at all possible. I have my wife rip out the women's underwear sections in Sears or Penney's catalogs. I won't watch certain TV shows because of sexual innuendo or gross sexual jokes or suggestive situations designed to stir up lust. I won't knowingly drive through certain parts of town where the sex industry flourishes. As I learn more about walking in the Spirit, I try to make a habit of keeping away from these sorts of situations, and thus to avoid potential entanglements with sin. I also refuse to stay alone in a hotel room that offers adult movies or that rents such videos. God in His Word has commanded us to take responsibility for the life-style choices we make.

As followers of the Lord Jesus Christ, we are at war with the world, the flesh, and the Devil. In our battle with the world, there are things we can change and things we can't. Most of the time when the world tempts us, it's a geographic temptation. If we change our immediate location, the temptation will diminish or go away. This is why Scripture commands us to "flee the evil desires of youth" (2 Timothy 2:22).

In Scripture Joseph is a hero who illustrates this principle. Genesis tells us that Joseph was a handsome man who worked as the chief slave in his master Potiphar's household. Genesis 39:6-12 says:

Now Joseph was well-built and handsome, and after a while his master's wife took notice of Joseph and said, "Come to bed with me!" . . . though she spoke to Joseph day after day, he refused to go to bed with her or even be with her. One day he went into the house to attend to his duties, and none of the household servants was inside. She caught him by his cloak and said, "Come to bed with me!" But he left his cloak in her hand and ran out of the house." (emphasis mine)

Joseph exemplifies what the Scriptures tell us to do when aggressive sexual temptation stares us in the face. He fled and so escaped. The Scriptures relate one of Joseph's conversations with this wayward wife in Genesis 39:8-9: "With me in charge, my master does not concern himself with anything in the house; everything he owns he has entrusted to my care. No one is greater in this house than I am. My master has withheld nothing from me except you, because you are his wife. How then could I do such a wicked thing and sin against God?" The key to Joseph's successfully handling this temptation was that he saw it from God's point of view. He understood that adultery was "wicked" and would break his master's trust. He was also deeply aware of the presence and holiness of God. He knew adultery is a "sin" against God; therefore he fled.

Joseph was true to his God while an exile in Egypt. The good hand of the Lord was clearly upon him. Whether in Potiphar's house or in jail or interpreting dreams, God prospered him. It is imperative that we believers remember who we are and whom we serve. We are exiles and sojourners in this world (1 Peter 2:11). The disciplines of fasting, prayer, and reading the Scriptures daily help me keep that in mind. From a warfare perspective, we must know when to retreat. It's not cowardly to say, "I don't want to go to that movie" or to tell your buddies, "I need to leave now." "Flee the evil desires of youth, and pursue righteousness, faith, love and peace, along with those who call on the Lord out of a pure heart" (2 Timothy 2:22). In our battle with the world, we must be aware of our surroundings and must be ready to change our environment in order to keep pure.

Another Navy story illustrates this point. Sam was a naval officer who was conscientious, moral, God-fearing, and pure. Sam worked hard to do his job right. The lives of men and millions of dollars of equipment were daily in his hands. He was responsible for vectoring jets, nearly empty of gas, to tanker jets, as well as directing the planes in time of war to their targets. When the officers in the ward room showed porn flicks, Sam had already determined not to defile himself; he would quietly walk out. Sometimes there would be jeers and a few critical comments, usually in jest but sometimes cutting and hurting, even questioning his virility. This really irked Sam, but these comments were not frequent. Sam had grown more and more comfortable with these men, and he felt they respected his values. He thought nothing of the "All Officers Mandatory Meeting" to be held at a club in the foreign port their ship was visiting, though Sam thought it curious that several men, including his Commanding Officer and Executive Officer, personally asked him if he was going to attend.

Sam arrived at the club, fighting through the crowds of prostitutes that lined the streets begging the sailors for a night's work. He enjoyed the smell of barbecued mystery meat, probably monkey. He held his breath as he approached the club, trying not to breathe the overwhelming stench of the open sewage ditch combined with the exhaust of hundreds of brightly colored jeeps, each spewing out exhaust diesel fumes.

When he arrived at the club, he found it dimly lit. Loud rock music was being sung by teenage girls who knew no English but had memorized the words from tapes. Sam spotted his CO and XO and could smell the booze and cigarette smoke that filled the air. Officers from his squadron were sitting around the perimeter of the room in booths, each with several women surrounding them. He ordered a Coke and waited for the meeting to start.

As soon as Sam arrived, there was a sense of excitement in the air. The Commanding Officer whistled loudly and motioned for the music to stop. Everyone clapped when the CO announced that the meeting would begin with a door prize to be won in a random drawing. With great fanfare, a bowl containing every officer's name on a separate slip of paper was brought to the CO. Whoever's name was drawn would win the prize.

To his excitement but later to his horror, Sam's name was called. He had won! But what had he won? From behind him, Sam heard cheers and yells from the men and the hookers. Sam was standing in the center of the room when a woman walked up to him and started dancing and doing a slow striptease, simultaneously trying to get Sam to join her in a mutual disrobing. His trusted companions were chanting, laughing, and cheering Sam and the hooker on.

As Sam realized that a hooker and her services were the prize he had won, he felt trapped and betrayed by those who he thought were friends who respected him. They knew he was a Christian. They knew he was a virgin and that he had tried to live a morally pure life. A flood of emotions welled up within him. He needed time to process what was happening, time to pray. His flesh was beginning to respond to what his eyes were seeing. He needed to flee, and he did. He ran out of the club, leaving the hooker dancing alone in the middle of the floor. He could hear the howls of laughter and the jeers from the officers in his squadron as he quickly walked away from the club and made his way back to the ship.

Proverbs 4:14-17 says:

Do not set foot on the path of the wicked or walk in the way of evil men. Avoid it, do not travel on it; turn from it and go on your way. For they cannot sleep till they do evil; they are robbed of slumber till they make someone fall. They eat the bread of wickedness and drink the wine of violence.

These men had made it their objective to cause Sam to stumble morally. They had plotted together to rig the door prize. They all contributed money to purchase the hooker. They rigged up a special meeting and falsely used a legal military order to lure Sam into the trap. And the only reason was to "make someone fall." But by the grace of God and because of Sam's courage and determination to remain sexually pure, their plan failed.

Another Navy story further illustrates this point. In the Spring of 1941, the mighty German battleship *Bismarck* left its berth from Nazi-occupied Norway and headed for the Atlantic Ocean. Its mission was to sink and disrupt Allied convoy operations supplying Britain with needed war supplies. The British Navy knew there were only four possible ways for the *Bismarck* to pass into the Atlantic from Norway and stationed ships in each passageway to locate and monitor her progress. The British ships *Suffolk* and *Norfolk* were in the northernmost passageway, moving in and out of a fog bank. When the fog cleared at one point, the *Norfolk* found the mighty ship *Bismarck* only six miles away and headed straight toward her. Since the *Bismarck's* guns were bigger and had a longer range than the *Norfolk's*, the British ship laid down a smoke screen and headed back into the fog bank as rapidly as possible. The *Bismarck* opened fire, narrowly missing the *Norfolk*. The *Norfolk* had acted properly when she fled since she was outgunned.

Romans 13:14 says, "Clothe yourselves with the Lord Jesus Christ, and do not think about how to gratify the desires of the sinful nature." We are not to play around with the flesh. We are not to see how close we can come to temptation and then escape. We are rather to discipline ourselves to stay far away from sexual temptation and, when necessary, to flee. Why? "The spirit is willing, but the body is weak" (Matthew 26:41).

The world is not a friendly place for the Christian who is seeking to keep pure. In America many advertisers use sex to make their products attractive. Whether it be milk or toothpaste or computers, sex sells. The Lord knows this. First Corinthians 5:9-11 says, "I have written you in my letter not to associate with sexually immoral people—not at all meaning the people of this world who are immoral, or the greedy and swindlers, or idolaters. In that case you would have to leave this world. But now I am writing you that you must not associate with anyone who calls himself a brother but is sexually immoral. . . ." God is not asking us to leave the planet, but He does want us to influence the world via pure, upright, and holy lives. He calls us to be beacon lights to the world.

The world is a hostile enemy to anyone who wants to keep pure. Recognizing this, we must discipline ourselves accordingly, staying close to Christ and relying on Him for courage and strength.

KEY PRINCIPLE

To experience sexual purity, we must exercise self-discipline, denying ourselves sinful indulgence and choosing again and again to do what is right, with God's help.

KEY VERSES

"In a large house there are articles not only of gold and silver, but also of wood and clay; some are for noble purposes and some for ignoble. If a man cleanses himself from the latter, he will be an instrument for noble purposes, made holy, useful to the Master and prepared to do any good work. Flee the evil desires of youth, and pursue righteousness, faith, love and peace, along with those who call on the Lord out of a pure heart" (2 Timothy 2:20-22).

DISCUSSION QUESTIONS

1. What you are doing to discipline yourself to keep pure? Discuss this with a Christian brother who could be a prayer partner with you as you battle for sexual purity.

2. What other steps do you need to take to guard yourself against moral failure? Be specific. Do you need to enlist others to help you take these steps (the Christian brother from question #1, your wife, etc.)?

3. Have you experienced an incident when you had to flee? What were the circumstances? How did others involved in the situation react to your departure? Did they understand the reasons for your decision? Do you feel it would be profitable to try to explain it to them?

4. If you have had an incident where you did not flee but failed, confess that to God and to the brother named above. Do you believe God can restore you and continue to help you grow in spiritual understanding and effective service? Talk to Him about it now.

CHAPTER TWELVE

The Discipline
of the Lord

Several years ago the USS *Enterprise*, while steaming in the open ocean off the coast of Southern California, struck Bishop's Rock, slicing a large gash in the hull of the ship. Bishop's Rock is a well-known navigational hazard, clearly marked on the charts or maps used by naval vessels. The Commanding Officer knew his ship was steaming in the area and had given specific instructions to steer well clear of the rock. But his watch standers got confused as to where they were located, and the rest is history.

It is a fact that when a ship strikes a rock, gashing a hole in the hull, it will take on water. Just as obvious, steer a ship into shallow water, and it will go aground. Just as certain is this: when we sin, there are consequences. Galatians 6:7-8 says, "Do not be deceived: God cannot be mocked. A man reaps what he sows. The one who sows to please his sinful nature, from that nature will reap destruction; the one who sows to please the Spirit, from the Spirit will reap eternal life."

Several years ago I made a trip to the eye doctor to have him

surgically remove a cyst from my eyelid. It was the fourth trip
within a year to remove a total of eight cysts. The treatment was
warm soaks, eyedrops, and an eye ointment to aid the healing process. First there was the agony of the cyst itself, causing even an
eye blink to be painful, then the pain of the removal of it. I also
had to use valuable time on five-minute warm soaks three to four
times a day. I also had to pay the cost of the medicine and of seeing the doctor numerous times over the course of the year. I found
myself asking, "Why me? Why do I have these cysts? And why
in my eyes?" The eye doctor said, "It's just one of those things."
But was it?

As I thought and prayed about this, the idea of God's discipline kept coming to mind. Could it be that God was allowing
these things to grow in my eyes as a means of physically disciplining me regarding my lack of self-control when I searched for
and looked at pornography? Hebrews 12:3-17 says:

> *Consider him who endured such opposition from sinful men,*
> *so that you will not grow weary and lose heart. In your*
> *struggle against sin, you have not yet resisted to the point of*
> *shedding your blood. And you have forgotten that word of*
> *encouragement that addresses you as sons: "My son, do not*
> *make light of the Lord's discipline, and do not lose heart*
> *when he rebukes you, because the Lord disciplines those he*
> *loves, and he punishes everyone he accepts as a son."*
> *Endure hardship as discipline; God is treating you as sons.*
> *For what son is not disciplined by his father? If you are not*
> *disciplined (and everyone undergoes discipline), then you*
> *are illegitimate children and not true sons. Moreover, we*
> *have all had human fathers who disciplined us and we*
> *respected them for it. How much more should we submit to*
> *the Father of our spirits and live! Our fathers disciplined us*
> *for a little while as they thought best; but God disciplines us*

for our good, that we may share in his holiness. No discipline seems pleasant at the time, but painful. Later on, however, it produces a harvest of righteousness and peace for those who have been trained by it. Therefore, strengthen your feeble arms and weak knees. "Make level paths for your feet," so that the lame may not be disabled, but rather healed. Make every effort to live in peace with all men and to be holy; without holiness no one will see the Lord. See to it that no one misses the grace of God and that no bitter root grows up to cause trouble and defile many. See that no one is sexually immoral, or is godless like Esau, who for a single meal sold his inheritance rights as the oldest son. Afterward, as you know, when he wanted to inherit this blessing, he was rejected. He could bring about no change of mind, though he sought the blessing with tears.

Verse 4 mentions a "struggle against sin." The fact is, sometimes when I felt a desire to view pornography, I didn't struggle— I was a willing participant. I felt sin was inevitable, that if the opportunity came to look at it, I'd fall, so why fight it? I believed, and in my view my experience proved, that it was only a matter of time before I'd stumble again. I figured I would yield to "ever-increasing wickedness" (Romans 6:19) until I would finally be "disqualified" from the battle (1 Corinthians 9:24-27). I feared that just as Esau was rejected by God, I would be too, with no chance to repent, even if I sought it with tears (Hebrews 12:16-17).

And then I started getting those cysts. Scripture teaches that God does indeed spank or discipline His children. The pain I have endured is for my good. "No discipline seems pleasant at the time, but painful. Later on, however, it produces a harvest of righteousness and peace for those who have been trained by it" (verse 11).

It is important to balance the truths of Scripture. Psalm 103:8-14 says:

The LORD is compassionate and gracious, slow to anger,
abounding in love. He will not always accuse, nor will he
harbor his anger forever; he does not treat us as our sins
deserve or repay us according to our iniquities. For as high
as the heavens are above the earth, so great is his love for
those who fear him; as far as the east is from the west, so
far has he removed our transgressions from us. As a father
has compassion on his children, so the LORD has compas-
sion on those who fear him; for he knows how we are
formed, he remembers that we are dust.

God does not punish believers for their sin. Jesus paid the
penalty for all our sin on the cross. But God does *discipline* His
children in order to conform them to the image of His son.

We need to be clear on this. God is not a heavenly ogre waiting to zap us every time we sin. Psalm 103 clearly shows God's
tender mercy and care for us. But we must also consider Hebrews
12. He deals with us compassionately but firmly at different levels of spiritual growth. I've walked with God for over twenty
years, and God has a higher expectation of me now than when I
first believed in Him. He expects me to stand in faith and to obey
what I know. And "God disciplines us for our good, that we may
share in his holiness" (verse 10). First Thessalonians 4:3 adds, "It
is God's will that you should be sanctified: that you should avoid
sexual immorality."

Instead of my medical condition being a cause for fear, it
should be a source of joy, for His discipline is a sure mark of His
love for me. As a result of His spanking me, I am more motivated
to pray more about maintaining personal purity. I now more often
pray, "And lead me not into temptation." I regularly ask God to
guard and protect me and to keep me away from pornography or

sensuous literature. I will always have the scars in my eyelids to remind me of the seriousness of this.

I am not saying that all physical affliction is caused directly by God or that it is all a result of personal sin. Jesus' comments in John 9:3 indicate otherwise. But God does sometimes work in this way (either doing it Himself or permitting the trial to happen) in order to assist our growth in holiness.

Consider the story of David, who after he had committed adultery with Bathsheba, tried to live a secret life. He hid his sin for months, then compounded his sin by trying to mask Bathsheba's subsequent pregnancy by having Uriah, her husband, come home from the battlefield in hopes he would have sexual relations with Bathsheba and think he was the child's father. When Uriah refused to sleep with his wife, David stealthily had Uriah killed on the battlefield. The plan worked to perfection from man's perspective. But God is a seeing God, and He was not going to let David get away with such unholy living. Second Samuel 11:27 says, "But the thing David had done displeased the LORD." In fact, David had committed a sin worthy of death. God sent Nathan, the prophet, to confront David, and when David was forced to face his sin, he immediately confessed and agreed with the charges. God's response to David via Nathan the prophet in 2 Samuel 12:13 was, "The LORD has taken away your sin. You are not going to die."

But at the same time, there were lasting consequences for David and his household because of that sexual fall. The sword never left David's house. The baby born to Bathsheba and David died. David's son Absalom rebelled against David, taking David's wives and having sexual relationships with them openly, fulfilling 2 Samuel 12:11.

What discipline has the Lord brought into your life to assist you in your struggle with sexual sin ? A broken relationship? A disease? A ruined reputation? Persistent guilt and shame? An unwanted pregnancy? "God cannot be mocked." If we play with sin, our loving Father will discipline us for our good, to train us so we will become more like Jesus. The book of Proverbs is very clear about the cause/effect nature of sexual sin. For example:

> *Her house [the adulteress] leads down to death and her paths to the spirits of the dead. None who go to her return or attain the paths of life.*
>
> *—2:18-19*

> *For the lips of an adulteress drip honey, and her speech is smoother than oil; but in the end she is bitter as gall, sharp as a double-edged sword. Her feet go down to death; her steps lead straight to the grave. She gives no thought to the way of life; her paths are crooked, but she knows it not. Now then, my sons, listen to me; do not turn aside from what I say. Keep to a path far from her, do not go near the door of her house, lest you give your best strength to others and your years to one who is cruel, lest strangers feast on your wealth and your toil enrich another man's house. At the end of your life you will groan, when your flesh and body are spent. You will say, "How I hated discipline! How my heart spurned correction! I would not obey my teachers or listen to my instructors. I have come to the brink of utter ruin in the midst of the whole assembly."*
>
> *—5:3-14*

> *For a man's ways are in full view of the LORD, and he examines all his paths. The evil deeds of a wicked man ensnare him; the cords of his sin hold him fast. He will die for lack of discipline, led astray by his own great folly.*
>
> *—5:21-23*

For these commands are a lamp, this teaching is a light, and the corrections of discipline are the way to life, keeping you from the immoral woman, from the smooth tongue of the wayward wife. Do not lust in your heart after her beauty or let her captivate you with her eyes, for the prostitute reduces you to a loaf of bread, and the adulteress preys upon your very life. Can a man scoop fire into his lap without his clothes being burned? Can a man walk on hot coals without his feet being scorched? So is he who sleeps with another man's wife; no one who touches her will go unpunished. Men do not despise a thief if he steals to satisfy his hunger when he is starving. Yet if he is caught, he must pay sevenfold, though it costs him all the wealth of his house. But a man who commits adultery lacks judgment; whoever does so destroys himself. Blows and disgrace are his lot, and his shame will never be wiped away; for jealousy arouses a husband's fury, and he will show no mercy when he takes revenge. He will not accept any compensation; he will refuse the bribe, however great it is.

—6:23-35

With persuasive words she led him astray; she seduced him with her smooth talk. All at once he followed her like an ox going to the slaughter, like a deer stepping into a noose till an arrow pierces his liver, like a bird darting into a snare, little knowing it will cost him his life. Now then, my sons, listen to me; pay attention to what I say. Do not let your heart turn to her ways or stray into her paths. Many are the victims she has brought down; her slain are a mighty throng. Her house is a highway to the grave, leading down to the chambers of death.

—7:21-27

If you have lived a lifestyle of sin and are suffering from the effects of that sin, there is hope. Repent and turn back to God. God will remove the discipline once you have been trained by it.

Even if you have AIDS or some other deadly disease from which you may eventually die, God can and will use you to His glory if you repent, seek Him with all your might, and do what He calls you to do. All of us who know Christ as Savior have a marvelous hope—the resurrection of our bodies to be with Jesus and live with Him forever. Isaiah 55:6-7 says, "Seek the LORD while he may be found; call on him while he is near. Let the wicked forsake his way and the evil man his thoughts. Let him turn to the LORD, and he will have mercy on him, and to our God, for he will freely pardon." And Philippians 3:20-21 says, "Our citizenship is in heaven. And we eagerly await a Savior from there, the Lord Jesus Christ, who, by the power that enables him to bring everything under his control, will transform our lowly bodies so that they will be like his glorious body."

KEY PRINCIPLE

Because God loves us, He disciplines us when we sin, to make us more like Jesus Christ.

KEY VERSES

"And you have forgotten that word of encouragement that addresses you as sons: 'My son, do not make light of the Lord's discipline, and do not lose heart when he rebukes you, because the Lord disciplines those he loves, and he punishes everyone he accepts as a son.' Endure hardship as discipline; God is treating you as sons. For what son is not disciplined by his father?" (Hebrews 12:5-7).

DISCUSSION QUESTIONS

1. What is the difference between discipline and punishment? Give an example of each in everyday life, in the church, in your own life.

2. Which of these does God do in the lives of His children—those who truly know Him through faith in Jesus Christ? Explain your answer. On what do you base this?

3. Has the Lord ever disciplined you for sexual impurity? Tell a Christian brother about this, including the end results in your walk with the Lord.

Dealing with Consequences and Casualties

In the Navy all sailors who work in the engineering and reactor spaces of a ship are required to memorize emergency casualty procedures. The instructions must be followed verbatim, and in the proper order, whenever a mishap or casualty occurs. These orders are designed to 1) minimize and/or stop damage to equipment; 2) minimize the effect of a casualty on the operations of the ship; 3) keep the casualty from spreading or getting worse; 4) protect people from danger; and 5) restore the plant to operating condition as soon as possible.

Teams of trainers drill each person on these casualty procedures until they not only know them completely but can execute them consistently. Often these procedures have as many as ten immediate action steps, with additional follow-up steps. The more complicated the casualty, the more complex the actions required to recover from it. For example, if there was a radioactive water spill, we had to take appropriate action (which we summarized with an acrostic—SWIMS).

Stop the spill. The first step is to keep the radioactive leak from getting any bigger.

Warn others. Whoever sees the spill would immediately start yelling, "Spill! Spill!" alerting others in the area not to walk through the water, causing the radiation to spread.

Isolate the area. The area is immediately roped off so others will not walk into the contaminated fluid.

Minimize exposure. Everyone involved in the cleanup was required to wear special clothing to minimize their exposure to harmful radiation

Secure ventilation. All vent fans were turned off to stop the spread of airborne contaminants.

Every time there was a spill, these steps were followed. Failure to follow them would cause potential injury to personnel.

There are also various emergency casualty procedures for sexual temptation. Knowing, then doing the appropriate action is crucial.

CASUALTY: IMPURE THOUGHTS CAUSED BY DEMONIC FORCES

The Scenario

You are praying or doing something spiritual in nature, and suddenly you find yourself thinking lustful thoughts even though you have not exposed yourself to a worldly source of temptation. Action must be taken as soon as you recognize you are thinking such thoughts.

Immediate Action Steps

1. *Quote and obey James 4:7,* " Submit yourselves, then, to God. Resist the devil, and he will flee from you." The attack is demonic in nature. Fleshly, flaming arrows of lust have pierced

your thought life. You were not in an evil or compromising situation. The temptations are suggestions from the evil one. (I am not suggesting that all battles with lust are battles with demons per se. We fight against the world, the flesh, and the Devil. But in this section we are speaking specifically of the war against demonically produced lust.)

2. *Resist.* Pray silently, or if no one is around say out loud, "I resist the Devil in the name and through the blood of Jesus Christ, my Savior. Because I am His child, these thoughts have no hold on my life. Father, please help me to think the thoughts You want me to think. I take these thoughts captive to obedience to You." Such a prayer is based on 2 Corinthians 10:3-5, "For though we live in the world, we do not wage war as the world does. The weapons we fight with are not the weapons of the world. On the contrary, they have divine power to demolish strongholds. We demolish arguments and every pretension that sets itself up against the knowledge of God, and *we take captive every thought to make it obedient to Christ*" (emphasis mine). This is the standard for which we are to strive.

3. Picture yourself on the cross and *reckon yourself dead to sin.* It is imperative that you recognize and acknowledge that even though the thoughts have been planted by an enemy, they are designed and can indeed lead the flesh into sinful thought and behavior. Meditate on Romans 6:1-4.

Follow-up Steps

4. If the thoughts persist, *repeat the first three steps.*

5. If you have dwelt on the lustful thoughts for any length of time, you have undoubtedly sinned by lusting about someone. *Ask*

the Father for forgiveness, claiming 1 John 1:9, "If we confess our sins, he is faithful and just and will forgive us our sins and purify us from all unrighteousness."

6. Satan will try his hardest to convince us we are not forgiven. If he is succeeding at this in your mind and soul, resist him by praying, "I thank You, Father, that what Satan is telling me is untrue, because You have said that if I confess my sins, You will forgive and cleanse me. And I know that Your Word is true."

7. If you are still being tempted, *continue to quote Scripture or start to sing a hymn or chorus*. Psalm 22:3 says that the Lord "inhabitest the praises of Israel" (KJV). The Devil desires us to worship him; praise to the Lord is intolerable to him. Singing God's praises also benefits you, helping you control your thoughts.

8. If the attack continues, *call a trusted friend and ask for prayer* (Ecclesiastes 4:9-10).

Discussion

These steps work because they are based on the truths of Scripture. But you will have to persist because the enemy is persistent. If you have never fought him before or if you have allowed lustful thinking to dwell in your mind, you may have to go through this procedure literally hundreds of times. When I first started, I would follow these steps twenty or thirty times an hour because my mind was filled with so many impure thoughts. But victory does come as we fight the battle in submission to the love and power of God.

CASUALTY: IMPURE THOUGHTS CAUSED BY
THE WORLD

The Scenario

The world entices us in many different ways. You may be watching a movie or TV show, and an immoral, lustful situation starts to develop, or the dialogue turns sexual and you begin thinking lustful thoughts.

Or perhaps you happen to drive into a certain area of town and are exposed to advertisements or stores that peddle lust to sell their products.

Or maybe you are in the company of someone telling lustful stories or dirty jokes.

Or you are tempted by phone sex.

Immediate Action Steps

1. You must change your environment. But how? *Flee.* If the TV is causing you to stumble, change the channel or turn off the television. If you are watching a movie at a theater, leave, or at least go get popcorn until that scene is over. Consider a self-imposed rating limit, such as not going to anything more than "PG" or "PG-13." But also realize that you can't trust the rating system of the movie industry. Read the reviews done by Christian, or at minimum moral, critics. If the film has nudity or sexual content, discipline yourself not to go to those movies. Romans 13:14 says, "Clothe yourselves with the Lord Jesus Christ, and do not think about how to gratify the desires of the sinful nature." Don't watch anything you wouldn't want your

grandmother, sister, or ten-year-old daughter or son to watch or to see you watching.

2. When you are being tempted, *start singing praise hymns and meditating on Scripture.* Psalm 1:2-3 says, "But his delight is in the law of the LORD, and on his law he meditates day and night. He is like a tree planted by streams of water, which yields its fruit in season and whose leaf does not wither. Whatever he does prospers." Ask the Lord to protect you, to guide your steps, and to get you out of the temptation as soon as possible. Post Scripture passages where you will see them—on the dashboard of your car, on the fridge, on your computer at work—to maintain an awareness that you need the Lord's help in the battle.

3. If a friend, coworker, or neighbor starts to tell lust-provoking stories or jokes, *walk away or take charge of the conversation.* Also, let that person know that you find such jokes offensive.

4. If you find yourself thinking lustful thoughts and can pinpoint the source, get rid of the source, then follow the procedures above. If you are tempted by phone sex, call the phone company and have them block out all phone numbers from your home that start with 900 as the area code, as well as all such services with some other prefix. Similarly, block out cable channels that cause you to stumble, and cut off adult movies available in a hotel room.

Follow-up Steps

5. *Examine your life* and see if any of what I have described in this section is a pattern of stumbling for you. If so, discipline yourself to change the patterns.

6. *Seek to know the Lord better and to do whatever He tells you to do.* This may mean making hard choices about your

lifestyle, your work, or your friends. "Do not . . . gratify the desires of the sinful nature."

Discussion

The solution for all the above situations is to *flee*—to change your location. Proverbs 6:27 says, "Can a man scoop fire into his lap without his clothes being burned?" We must get away from the source of temptation as quickly as possible. "The spirit is willing, but the body is weak" (Matthew 26:41).

CASUALTY: KNOWING AHEAD OF TIME OF POTENTIAL EXPOSURE TO SEXUAL TEMPTATION

The Scenario

Perhaps your work requires you to travel, and you often stay in hotels that show adult movies.

Or clients take you to bars and/or other tempting situations.

Or you travel overseas to other cultures with standards of behavior even lower than in post-Christian America.

Maybe your roommate or your wife will be gone for a period of time, and you will be home alone.

Immediate Action Steps

1. *Fast and pray, and recruit others to pray for you.* In Matthew 4 we read that before Jesus was tempted by the Devil, He fasted and prayed for forty days. Several weeks before I saw my first X-rated video, during a devotional time, the Lord led

me to fast and pray against temptation. I disobeyed, and as a result when the temptation came, I did not have the strength to resist. The Lord instructed us to pray, "And lead us not into temptation" for a reason.

2. *Develop a purity battle plan*, and take practical steps ahead of time such as:

3. *Call the hotel ahead of time*, and ask if they offer adult movies afterhours. If so, ask if the service can be blocked from your room. If they cannot do that, call around until you find a hotel that is purity safe. If you can't find a hotel that doesn't push pornography, ask if you can have a room without a TV. If they say no, ask if you can have the hotel maintenance man remove the TV from your room during your stay. You may have to pay a small fee for this, but that's better than staining your soul or losing sleep because you're fighting temptation.

4. *If necessary, remove the TV and/or video recorder or cable from your home*. If you have cable, you can have selected channels deleted. Usually there is a one-time fee for this. Our family had MTV and several other channels removed from our cable. One man I know put his TV in the shed outside their house. They bring it inside only when he and his wife both agree to watch a specific program.

5. *Recruit prayer support prior to your trip*. Tell trusted friends, a support group, or your wife what to pray. Tell them what area you are tempted in, and ask them to specifically ask you about that area upon your return.

6. *Every night call home or call a buddy*—someone who will hold you accountable. Pray with your friend over the phone.

7. *Set objectives for your free time*. Seek to establish routines. Bring a book to read, a Bible study to do, letters to write, a pro-

ject to work on—something to occupy your time so you don't drift into temptation.

Follow-up Steps

8. Upon your return *set up an accountability session* with your spouse, support group, or trusted friend, those who will ask you the hard questions that must be asked. (For more on accountability, see the next chapter.)
9. If you travel frequently to the same areas or cities, *develop a network of supporters and Christian friends in the areas away from home*.

Discussion

Again, you must be alert to the wiles and ways of temptation and aware of your own weaknesses. I have done a lot of traveling in my work and have watched hundreds of men beginning to succumb to temptation at airport newsstands and elsewhere by looking at pornography. It is so easy to rationalize to ourselves, "No one knows you here. Go ahead and look. It won't hurt anybody. No one will find out." In this way we exclude God from our thinking and ignore His ever-watchful eye and presence. We think we have a "secret life," but God sees it all.

CASUALTY: YOU HAVE OFFENDED ANOTHER PERSON

Because this and the following sexual casualties affect more than just ourselves, scriptural principles of reconciliation and conscience must be understood and practiced. As you pray and seek the Lord's help when your sin involves another person, ask for wisdom (James 1:5) and the grace to obey what the Lord reveals to you (Hebrews 4:16).

Reconciliation. Jesus said, "If your brother sins against you, go and show him his fault, just between the two of you. If he listens to you, you have won your brother over. But if he will not listen, take one or two others along, so that 'every matter may be established by the testimony of two or three witnesses.' If he refuses to listen to them, tell it to the church; and if he refuses to listen even to the church, treat him as you would a pagan or a tax collector" (Matthew 18:15-17). In Matthew 5:23-24 Jesus says, "Therefore, if you are offering your gift at the altar and there remember that your brother has something against you, leave your gift there in front of the altar. First go and be reconciled to your brother; then come and offer your gift." These two passages clearly show that when there is an offense between people, whoever recognizes the offense is to take the first step toward reconciliation. Whether you were the victim or the perpetrator, you need to take the initiative to ensure reconciliation.

Conscience. In 1 Timothy 1:18-19 Paul said, "Timothy, my son . . . fight the good fight, holding on to faith and a good conscience. Some have rejected these and so have shipwrecked their faith." In Acts 24:16 the apostle adds, "So I strive always to keep my conscience clear before God and man." As we spend time in the Word of God and learn the heart and desires of our Father, our conscience acts as an impartial judge of our actions and motives. Failure to listen to our conscience can lead to a shipwrecked faith. We sometimes do not have peace about a situation or a person because of the nagging voice of conscience. Obey the Scriptures, and be sensitive to your conscience as long as it is informed by the Word of God. *Honesty, Morality, and Conscience* by Jerry White (NavPress, 1988) provides a valuable discussion of this important topic.

Guidance. In Psalm 32:8-9 God tells us, "I will instruct you and teach you in the way you should go; I will counsel you and watch over you. Do not be like the horse or the mule, which have no understanding but must be controlled by bit and bridle." Romans 8:14 says, "Those who are led by the Spirit of God are sons of God." As we seek to obey the Father and submit to His will for our lives, He will guide and direct us.

Our overall goal should not be to keep our sin a secret but rather reconciliation with both God and others—a holy life with a clear conscience before God and man. Sexual sin is serious, but it is not the end of the world for the believer.

Following these principles from Scripture will help us walk in peace and purity. Ken Sandi, in his book *The Peacemaker*, lists the seven A's of *confession*. These steps are useful for those who have committed sexual sin against another person but now desire reconciliation:

1. *Address everyone involved.* If you offended ten people, then speak to all ten.

2. *Avoid the words: if, but and maybe.* These words lessen the extent of your involvement and shift blame to the other person.

3. *Admit specifically.* State exactly what you did that was sinful or wrong.

4. *Apologize.* Use the words, "I was wrong for . . ." Don't say, "I'm sorry" and leave it at that. It may mean you

were sorry for getting caught and not sorry for the hurt
your actions caused.

5. *Accept the consequences.* The other person may not
   choose to forgive you. Restitution may be required. In
   the area of sexual sin, it may mean going to jail, or
   being formally charged with a crime. It may mean recognizing that you are the father of a child and the subsequent moral, Biblical and legal obligations that
   entails.

6. *Alter your behavior.* Stop doing the behavior that violated the commands of Scripture and gave you a guilty
   conscience.

7. *Ask for forgiveness.* Ask the person you offended to
   forgive you. You cannot demand this. The other person may choose not to forgive you. You have done
   your part. Ask the Lord to help the other person to
   appropriate the grace to not be bitter and harbor
   resentment.

Immediate Action Steps

1. *Confess your sin to the Lord,* asking for forgiveness. Read and
   pray through 1 John 1:9 and Psalm 51. I don't want to minimize
   your sin, but it can be encouraging to know that you are not the
   first to fall. David committed adultery and then murder to cover
   his tracks; but he also paid a high price for his sin. When you
   commit sexual sin, you are stained. You can ask for forgiveness,
   but you probably won't *feel* forgiven. But God said you are forgiven if you confess. So are you going to believe God's Word
   or your feelings? At the same time, though God forgives you,
   there will still be consequences from your sin.

2. *Accept from the Lord's hand whatever discipline He brings.* It is a spiritual law that you reap what you sow (Galatians 6:7). It is true that He does not deal with us according to our sin or repay us according to our iniquity (Psalm 103:10). But it is also true that "the Lord disciplines those he loves, and he punishes everyone he accepts as a son" (Hebrews 12:6). How and when He disciplines us is His choice. He does not always deal with us immediately. At such times God's kindness is meant to lead us to repentance (Romans 2:4). You may have sex only one time but get someone pregnant. You may have sex one time and get AIDS or some other sexually transmitted disease. You may also be promiscuous, yet escape disease or pregnancy. What happens to you as a result of sexual sin is entirely up to the Lord. You can choose to sin, but you cannot choose the results of your sin. Our God is sovereign, and He does what He pleases (Psalm 115:3).

   Many sexual sins are not only sins against an individual but also against society. That is, some sexual sins not only break God's law but man's as well. If that is true in your case, God may direct you to turn yourself in to the police. The victim of your sexual sin may choose to press charges, and you may have to go to court and eventually prison to pay the penalty of your sin against society. God may be gracious and move the judge to give you a suspended sentence or probation. Or the victim may not choose to press charges. Only God knows what will happen; whatever He decides or allows is just. The question is, what price are you willing to pay for a clean conscience?

3. *Let the Lord direct you regarding whether or not to seek reconciliation with the offended person.* If He leads you to do so, follow the steps listed above for reconciliation.

Follow-up Steps

4. *Remember, you cannot dictate or control another person's response*. The person you offended may be in a state of denial or may angrily accuse you. You must obey the Lord and do what He commands you to do.

CASUALTY:POSSIBLE DISEASE

If you think you have a disease because of your sexual sin, get tested for it. Even if you don't think you have a disease, but you have been living a morally loose life, get tested for HIV.

Immediate Action Steps

1. *See your family doctor or go to a public health clinic*. Testing is done confidentially and, at a clinic, often free of charge.
2. *Spend much time in prayer and the Word*, drawing close to the Lord.

Follow-up Steps

3. *Tell a trusted friend or your pastor* about the situation. Ecclesiastes 4:9-10 says, "Two are better than one. . . . If one falls down, his friend can help him up. But pity the man who falls and has no one to help him up!"
4. If you do have a disease, and you are a true believer in Christ, *remember that your body is still a temple of God*. Taking care of your body is a stewardship issue.

5. *If you do have a disease, tell your partner or partners.* They may not know they are infected. If you know from whom you got the disease and that person knew he or she was infected and told you a lie in order to have sex, you have been doubly deceived, the first lie being that having sex outside the boundaries of marriage is satisfying or fulfilling. In such a situation you might be bitter toward that person; but you will not be spiritually whole before God as long as you shelter bitterness or unforgiveness in your heart.

6. *Follow the steps of reconciliation* related previously.

Discussion

Having a disease and not getting treated could lead to a deteriorating physical condition quicker than need be. Not having a disease but living your life like you have one amounts to living your life under the premise of a lie. Having a sexually transmitted disease is a heavy burden, but it is not the end of the world. Thousands of people have one of the over thirty different sexually transmitted diseases and yet lead productive, godly lives, through God's grace and love.

CASUALTY: IF A PARTNER HAS BECOME PREGNANT

Immediate Action Steps

1. *Ask God for guidance.*

2. *Do not further compound the sin by encouraging or paying for an abortion.* If you will not marry the woman or she will not

marry you or marriage is not possible because one of you is married already, the decision as to what to do with the child is out of your hands, given the current legal climate.

3. But you can *beseech the Lord for the life of that little one and for wisdom for the mother as she decides what she should do with the baby.* You can urge the mother to have the baby and relinquish the child to you, but legally the decision may be hers. If she decides to keep the baby, as the biological father of that baby you have a biblical and moral obligation to provide financial, spiritual, and emotional support to the child and, if she is willing, to the mother.

4. *If neither of you desires to keep the baby, give the baby up for adoption.* There are thousands of Christian couples who long to have a baby but for various reasons are unable to conceive. Your child would be a wonderful gift to one of those couples.

Follow-up Steps

5. For further information and help, *contact your local crisis pregnancy center.* You can find one by looking in the Yellow Pages of the phone book under "Abortion Alternatives."

6. *Seek godly counsel.* Talk to your pastor or some other mature Christian whom you respect and trust. But when you speak with them, be honest; don't sugarcoat the situation or hide your part in the sin that has occurred.

7. *Help the woman who is bearing your child.* She is in crisis and needs compassion. Find help for her emotionally and if need be financially. She will be under intense pressure to abort the baby. Neither you or she should rush into a hasty decision.

8. *Accept your full responsibility to support your child as much as is right and however God directs.* A lot of men, even some Christian men, are irresponsible, deadbeat dads. Such behavior discredits the name of Christ and must be completely avoided.

9. In saying this, I recognize that sometimes the fatherhood of a child to be born is not clear. *You can have tests done to verify that you are indeed the biological father.* If you are not the biological father, you have no legal obligation to provide for the child. However, God may still lead you to be involved in helping this woman in other ways. If you indeed had sex with her, you did in fact sin and must deal with that reality, though compassion is still appropriate. It is not sufficient to say, "Keep warm and well fed" when she has needs. Furthermore, you must guard yourself lest you be tempted to sexually sin with this woman again.

CASUALTY: YOU ARE HAVING AN AFFAIR OR HAVE COMMITTED ADULTERY

Immediate Action Steps

1. *Break off the relationship at once.* Flee the relationship; otherwise you will likely continue the sinful behavior.

2. *Resist temptation and reckon yourself dead to sin.* Follow the steps for resisting and reckoning that we discussed earlier.

3. *Ask the Lord for forgiveness.* Then, relying on His help, live a pure life and reconcile with others wherever there is the opportunity.

4. *Seek counseling from a mature brother or your pastor.*

5. *Seek close communion with the Lord, obey what He tells you to do, and listen to your conscience.* Once you have gone the way of adultery, your emotions are so involved that you are unable to clearly discern guidance from the Scriptures. Thus it is imperative that you allow God to restore you. "Therefore, I urge you, brothers, in view of God's mercy, to offer your bodies as living sacrifices, holy and pleasing to God—this is your spiritual act of worship. Do not conform any longer to the pattern of this world, but be transformed by the renewing of your mind. Then you will be able to test and approve what God's will is—his good, pleasing and perfect will" (Romans 12:1-2).

6. *Plead with God for mercy and wisdom for all parties concerned.*

Follow-up Steps

7. *Spend time with the Lord, asking Him to help you discern what led you into the affair in the first place.*

8. *Develop a purity battle plan to avoid similar situations in the future.*

Discussion

When you married your wife, you probably held the ceremony in a church, before a pastor, and vowed to God and your wife before many witnesses to be faithful sexually to her "until death do you part." But you have broken your vows to God and to your wife. What now? Should you tell your spouse or not?

The argument against telling your wife may include the following reasons: 1) she would kill me; 2) she would never forgive me; 3) she would hold it against me for the rest of my life; or 4) she would divorce me. Some or all of these may actually happen. There are many Christian books written on the topic of divorce, and most would say that adultery is a biblical ground for divorce. Jesus Himself says in Matthew 5:32, "But I tell you that anyone who divorces his wife, *except for marital unfaithfulness*, causes her to become an adulteress, and anyone who marries the divorced woman commits adultery" (emphasis mine). But divorce is not always the answer and, though allowed, is not required. With Christ's help, there can be forgiveness and reconciliation.

The argument for telling your wife about your sin may include some of the following reasons: 1) you desire to have a clear conscience; 2) you have wronged her and want her forgiveness; or 3) you want to continue being married to her because you love her and made a commitment to her that you still want to keep.

As you seek the Lord's direction in these matters, He will show you what to do. Do not presume that your wife could not or would not forgive you. God offers much grace to all who call upon Him, and He is able to bring a turnaround in the most impossible situations. My wife and I have counseled many couples where one partner has been sexually unfaithful to his or her spouse. In each case trust had been broken; but in each case where full confession, repentance, and forgiveness occurred, the marriage survived. Even then all bear the painful consequences of infidelity, but both partners continue to work on trust and avoiding the relational problems that contributed to the sin in the first place. With God, there is always hope. Love "always hopes" (1 Corinthians 13:7).

CASUALTY: YOU HAVE RAPED SOMEONE

Immediate Action Steps

1. *Pray and confess your sin to God.*
2. *Spend quality time in His presence and ask Him for wisdom* as to what you should do next.

Follow-up Steps

3. *Seek counsel* by talking to your pastor or a godly, trusted friend.
4. *Do not seek out your victim by yourself.* The last thing a rape victim wants is to come face to face with her rapist again, especially without warning. The victim has suffered much trauma and will probably need professional counseling. *Ask a pastor or other spiritual leader to pray for you and counsel you and possibly go on your behalf.* The Lord will guide you as you seek Him.
5. If the Lord leads you to do so, *follow the steps to reconciliation* discussed earlier.
6. Rape is not only a crime against one woman—it is a crime against society. The consequences of this sin may include going to court, having a criminal record, and/or serving time in prison. *By voluntarily confessing and making restitution, you will be paying your debt not only to your victim but to society.* In addition, the legal system may then be very lenient. (But don't confess just to lessen the penalty; rather, acknowledge your sin for the sake of truthfulness and godliness.) Rather than living a lie, always fearing discovery, be like the

apostle Paul in Acts 24:16: "So I strive always to keep my conscience clear before God and man."

Discussion

Many women are molested or raped in our nation. So there are a lot of men with guilty consciences. Sadly, some of them even claim to be or actually are followers of Jesus Christ, though they have not dealt with this issue in their lives. As children of the King, we have the opportunity to live our lives free from sin—being not only pardoned from the guilt of past iniquity, but being presently able through Christ to triumph over the power of present sin.

If you have raped or molested someone and have not acknowledged your wickedness, even as a believer you could never look that person in the eye with a clear conscience. I exhort you to repent and to forsake the past, so the enemy of your soul can no longer have a foothold on you.

CASUALTY: YOU HAVE BEEN THE VICTIM OF INCEST

Immediate Action Steps

1. *Seek help from a qualified Christian counselor.*
2. *Ask God for wisdom as to what to do and how to possibly reconcile with your relative.*
3. *Talk to your pastor and/or support group*, possibly an incest/molestation support group. Through such a group you can find healing and reconciliation.

Follow-up Steps

4. *Read Dan Allender's The Wounded Heart—Hope for Adult Victims of Childhood Sexual Abuse* (NavPress, 1990). This book provides wise suggestions and counsel. Another book some have found valuable is *A Door of Hope* by Jan Frank (Nelson/Word, 1993).

CASUALTY: YOU HAVE COMMITTED INCEST

Immediate Action Steps

1. *Talk to your pastor and/or support group.* If the victim was very young, he or she may be traumatized and may have wiped the memory out of his or her conscious mind. In such a case you will need special guidance and wisdom.
2. *Seek the Lord's will step by step in fervent, honest prayer.* Be willing to do whatever the Lord tells you to do.

Follow-up Steps

3. *Read Dan Allender's The Wounded Heart—Hope for Adult Victims of Childhood Sexual Abuse* (NavPress, 1990).

Discussion

If the victim has been traumatized (which is almost always the case), it will be harmful to approach that person without considering what is best for him or her. You may need to go to the parents or to ask a Christian brother to act as an intermediary.

CASUALTY: YOU ARE A HOMOSEXUAL OR HAVE LUSTFUL DESIRES TOWARD OTHER MEN

Immediate Action Steps

1. *Flee.* Break off all immoral sexual contacts.
2. *Reckon yourself dead to sin.* Follow the steps described when we discussed the first casualty.
3. *Resist temptation* following the steps described when we discussed the first two casualties.

Follow-up Steps

4. *Tell a trusted friend, pastor, or support group.*
5. *Contact Exodus International* at 415-454-1017. This organization was formed to meet the needs of people who struggle with this sin.
6. *Memorize key passages of Scripture* cited throughout this book and in the appendix.
7. *Read Coming Out of Homosexuality by Bob Davies and Lori Rentzel* (InterVarsity Press, 1993).

Discussion

Recognize that, like others who have committed sexual sin, you have believed some lies. No matter what you've been told or what you prefer to believe, God did not create you as a homosexual. Your same-sex desires come from habitual wrong thinking. You have trained yourself to lust mentally and to desire men instead of women. The good news is, just because you are homosexual does not mean you have to stay that way. You have gone aside from God's intentions for you, but He can put you back on the right path. First Corinthians 6:9-11 says:

> *Do you not know that the wicked will not inherit the king-*
> *dom of God? Do not be deceived: Neither the sexually*
> *immoral nor idolaters nor adulterers nor male prostitutes*
> *nor homosexual offenders nor thieves nor the greedy nor*
> *drunkards nor slanderers nor swindlers will inherit the*
> *kingdom of God. And that is what some of you were. But*
> *you were washed, you were sanctified, you were justified*
> *in the name of the Lord Jesus Christ and by the Spirit of*
> *our God.*

If you are homosexual, take courage. "That is what some of you were. But you were washed, you were sanctified . . ." The congregation in Corinth included former homosexuals. They left that lifestyle, and you can too. That may mean severing friendships that cause you to stumble. It certainly means reprogramming your mind to think God's thoughts about masculinity, purity, gratefulness, obedience, discipline, and much more. Perhaps you have tried and tried again in your own strength to leave a homosexual lifestyle, and you may feel that change is impossible. But through God's help and the power of the Holy Spirit *you can be free!*

I encourage you to follow the principles in this book. Everywhere that lust for women is mentioned, just put "men" in place of "women." I also urge you to seek and accept the support of people with whom you feel comfortable and "who call on the Lord out of a pure heart" (2 Timothy 2:22). Every man who struggles with sexual sin needs support, and that includes you.

CASUALTY: YOU ARE INVOLVED IN SEXUAL SIN
AND YOU RECOGNIZE IT AS SIN

The Scenario

Perhaps you are in bed with someone or are involved in an act of sexual sin.

Or you are in the process of seducing someone, and the Holy Spirit gets your attention.

Immediate Action Steps

1. *Ask God for the grace and strength needed to immediately stop what you are doing. Ask Him for the courage to obey Him,* even if that makes you look foolish to your partner.
2. *Flee the area.* Grab your clothes and get out of there. Joseph, when Potiphar's wife grabbed him, left his cloak behind and ran. She then falsely accused him of rape, and Joseph was imprisoned as a result. But through all of that he did not give in to sexual temptation or dishonor the God of holiness.
3. *Avoid that person or situation in the future,* especially when there is no one else around.
4. *Follow the steps involved in warring against impure thinking, resisting the Devil, and reckoning yourself dead to sin.*
5. *You may eventually need to reconcile with the person with whom you were involved.*

Follow-up Steps

6. *Discern how you got into the immoral situation in the first place,* so you can, with God's help, avoid a similar fall in the future.

7. *Develop a purity battle plan and follow it. If you already have one, revise it if necessary, but keep carrying it out.*
8. *Confess your sin to Christian brothers* whom you trust and who understand the issues involved. Ask them to hold you accountable and to pray for you.

CASUALTY: YOU DESIRE TO MASTURBATE

The Scenario

You decide you want to masturbate, then begin to make your plans.

Immediate Action Steps

1. *Ask the Lord to fill you with His Spirit,* to take control of your life at this moment and work His will. Romans 8:12-13 says, "Therefore, brothers, we have an obligation—but it is not to the sinful nature, to live according to it. For if you live according to the sinful nature, you will die; but if by the Spirit you put to death the misdeeds of the body, you will live."
2. *Reckon and resist.* Go through the steps outlined previously, reckoning yourself dead to sin and resisting demonic temptation by consciously submitting to God. Mentally review Romans 6 and James 4:7, entreating God to help you control your thoughts.

Follow-up Steps

3. *Discipline yourself to spend time in the Word and prayer regularly.*

4. *Ask the Lord to show you why you have wrong desires.* Ask Him to reveal any burdens or anxieties you are carrying, then give them back to Him.

5. *If you are married, tell your wife you are especially struggling with sexual desire at this time.* Ask her for her help by making herself available to you for sexual satisfaction. First Corinthians 7:1-6 says:

> *Now for the matters you wrote about: It is good for a man not to marry. But since there is so much immorality, each man should have his own wife, and each woman her own husband. The husband should fulfill his marital duty to his wife, and likewise the wife to her husband. The wife's body does not belong to her alone but also to her husband. In the same way, the husband's body does not belong to him alone but also to his wife. Do not deprive each other except by mutual consent and for a time, so that you may devote yourselves to prayer. Then come together again so that Satan will not tempt you because of your lack of self-control. I say this as a concession, not as a command.*

6. *Remove anything from your home that causes you to want to sin sexually*—books, magazines, videos, etc.

7. *Call a Christian friend with whom you can fellowship during this time of temptation.*

8. *Go for a run or engage in some other type of strenuous exercise.*

9. *If you yield to the temptation, confess as soon as possible, and don't dwell on it.* You will feel guilty because you have given in to your flesh and have obeyed its desires, but don't keep punishing yourself about it; instead, rejoice in the cleansing, forgiving power of the blood of Jesus Christ. Renew your fellowship with God and again reckon yourself dead to sin.

CASUALTY: YOU STRUGGLE WITH CYBERSEX—
IMMORALITY THROUGH THE INTERNET

Immediate Action Steps

1. At a moment when you are fighting this battle, *turn off the computer.*
2. *Go through the steps of resisting, reckoning, and fleeing* as discussed previously.

Follow-up Steps

3. If you are using a commercial service that does not screen out pornography, *change companies.*
4. *Develop a purity battle plan that includes accepting accountability for yourself.*
5. *If need be, get rid of all ability to access the Internet.*
6. *If need be, get rid of your computer.*

Discussion

In Matthew 5:29 Jesus said, "If your right eye causes you to sin, gouge it out and throw it away. It is better for you to lose one part of your body than for your whole body to be thrown into hell." Romans 13:14 adds, "Clothe yourselves with the Lord Jesus Christ, and do not think about how to gratify the desires of the sinful nature." We must strive after holiness and work hard for it, relying on God's help but making an effort ourselves as well. If a computer or TV or video or anything else the world has to offer hurts my relationship with God, I need to take action. Either I put it to death, or it will eventually shipwreck my faith and endanger my walk with Christ and perhaps even my physical life.

We must choose—we must persevere—we must fight! "Be strong in the Lord and in his mighty power. Put on the full armor of God so that you can take your stand against the devil's schemes" (Ephesians 6:10-11).

KEY PRINCIPLE

Knowing and executing emergency casualty procedures for various specific situations is essential if we are to regain and maintain sexual purity.

KEY VERSES

"Therefore, brothers, we have an obligation—but it is not to the sinful nature, to live according to it. For if you live according to the sinful nature, you will die; but if by the Spirit you put to death the misdeeds of the body, you will live" (Romans 8:12-13). "If we confess our sins, he is faithful and just and will forgive us our sins and purify us from all unrighteousness" (1 John 1:9).

DISCUSSION QUESTIONS

1. Which of the struggles discussed in this chapter are currently yours? Which of these battle plans do you need to act on? Will you begin today? What is at stake?

2. Can you think of or have you used additional tactics for triumph in the battle for sexual purity? Which ones were effective?

Why? What measures have you taken that did not produce victory? Why was this?

3. Are you currently experiencing victory or defeat in your fight against the temptation to engage in sexual sin? What can you do to win the battle more often?

___

CHAPTER FOURTEEN

Battle Partners

Every ship in the Navy has to go through various inspections to ensure readiness. Each room or compartment must be both airtight and watertight. The engines are tested. The personnel running the engines are questioned to be sure they are competent. The damage control lockers are inventoried to make sure all required emergency equipment is present and in top working shape. The ship's missiles and guns are fired and the crews trained for accuracy. Each year there are literally thousands of inspections of a ship and her crew. As the expression says, "You don't get what you expect, but what you inspect."

Ships and crews are held accountable for their knowledge, training, and performance. Similarly, Christian men need to hold each other accountable in their walk with the Lord, especially in the area of sexual purity. How can we do this? What makes accountability work?

Chuck Swindoll, in his book *Dropping Your Guard*, stresses four things: vulnerability, availability, teachability, and honesty. To summarize his thoughts, we must be open to the loving probing of another's questions. When a brother needs to talk, he requires someone to whom he can pour out his heart. When someone is trying to hold you accountable for your actions and asks you a question, you must answer honestly. And you must be willing to learn from a brother. These are especially crucial in our mutual battle for sexual purity. "Therefore confess your sins to each other and pray for each other so that you may be healed. The prayer of a righteous man is powerful and effective" (James 5:16).

The following letter came to me from an airline pilot who was struggling with sexual purity. Because he travels a lot and is away from his wife about a third of the time, he faces a lot of temptation, particularly from TV. When he asked me to hold him accountable, I asked him to develop a purity plan to use when he traveled. Several weeks later he wrote:

> Dear Bob,
>   I promised you a written "plan of attack for purity," so here it is.
>   1. Memorize Romans 8:1-17.
>   2. Communicate daily with my wife when on the road via telephone and be held accountable by her (best time 9-10 P.M.).
>   3. Disconnect cable TV with front desk if that option exists.
>   4. Throw away any TV/cable guide that I come across.
>   5. When tempted: sit down and recite/write Romans 8:1-17 and pray.
>   6. Pray daily for victory (twice: once in the morning and once in the evening).

This man is serious about living a pure life and being pleasing and useful to the Lord. He brought his wife in on his temptations and confessed to her his past failures when traveling. At first his wife was hurt, angry, and upset. But over a period of time she came to understand that her husband's struggles were not a reflection on her ability to please him sexually or a rejection of her or her appearance. His struggles were primarily between the Lord and himself. She also came to realize that she could either aid her husband's attempts to live in purity or contribute to her husband's stumbling. She chose to help her husband be obedient to the Lord. This set him free to enlist his wife's help and to be honest with her in his struggles. It also brought him his best prayer and accountability partner. As he confided in her about the sexual temptations in his life, their intimacy increased.

Sadly, such husband-and-wife teamwork in the battle for sexual purity is rare. Many men I disciple say their wives have no awareness of their moral struggles. Other men who hinted to their wives about their battles were greeted with disbelief. One wife said to her husband after hearing the report of a Christian man who was battling with pornography, "I just can't understand how a Christian man could struggle with that!" Her own husband had for weeks been praying for the courage to confide in his wife about his own struggles, but her naiveté shut the door. Other women go into depression or conclude *they* are the problem—"If only I were prettier . . . weighed less . . . were sexier." All of these may be factors but usually aren't. A man could be married to a Marilyn Monroe-type woman, pretty in face and form, and have sex with her every day, yet still be tempted!

It is the nature of man to gravitate toward sin. His eyes are never satisfied (Proverbs 27:20). The world is constantly offering enticements to sin. Some people even deliberately try to get a man who desires to live a pure life to stumble and fall. Satan is con-

stantly prowling around like a roaring lion, looking for someone
to devour (1 Peter 5:8).

God never intended for men to fight the battle for sexual
purity alone. If wives only understood this, how much easier it
would be for husbands to stay pure. First Corinthians 7:2-6 is not
in the Bible by accident:

> *But since there is so much immorality, each man should
> have his own wife, and each woman her own husband. The
> husband should fulfill his marital duty to his wife, and like-
> wise the wife to her husband. The wife's body does not
> belong to her alone but also to her husband. In the same
> way, the husband's body does not belong to him alone but
> also to his wife. Do not deprive each other except by mutual
> consent and for a time, so that you may devote yourselves
> to prayer. Then come together again so that Satan will not
> tempt you because of your lack of self-control.*

If you are married, what role is your wife playing in your
struggle for purity? Does she even know about it? Does she know
when the vulnerable times of your life are? Does she feel free to
ask you about your thought life? Are you hiding something from
your wife that she should know about?

The one factor that has sometimes kept me from open, honest communication with my wife about these matters is *fear*. Here
is a list of fears that I have had or that other men have expressed
to me:

> Fear she will get angry and yell at me.
> Fear she will reject me.
> Fear she will go into depression.
> Fear she will lose respect for me.
> Fear she will not want to have sex with me.

Fear she will think I don't love her.
Fear she will think I don't see her as attractive.
Fear she will think she is inadequate in bed.
Fear she will leave me.
Fear she will tell her friends and they will hate me.
Fear she will tell her family and they will lose respect
   for me.
Fear she just won't understand.
Fear she will think I am not normal or that I am a pervert.

If you are married and are struggling with impurity and your wife is not on board with you, ask God to help you know how to solicit her assistance and support. She may need to be taught about men and their sex drive. Pray that she would read the appropriate books or that God would bring a wise, older woman into her life to counsel her and be a resource for her. It is helpful for a husband and wife to attend together a marriage conference where sexuality is discussed from a candid, godly, biblical perspective.

When I agree to regularly meet with a man for accountability purposes, I always ask the hard questions about this area of his life, questions such as:

Are you struggling with sexually impure thoughts?
Are you living a life of immorality?
Do you struggle with masturbation?
If married, are you content with the physical relationship
   with your wife?
Is your wife content with the physical relationship?
Do you struggle with homosexual thoughts?
Do you struggle with pornography?
Are you struggling with any other sexual sin?
Have you been honest with me?

Most of the men I have met with over the years want account-ability in this area of their life. They also want accountability in other areas, such as their devotional life, use of money, use of time, and character issues such as anger, impatience, or pride. But the area of sexuality seems to be the Waterloo for many men. If a man has walked with God for a period of time and knows the Word but is unfruitful in the harvest field of men's souls, I inspect this area first. Sadly, this is one of the key areas of failure that keep men from being fruitful or productive in God's kingdom.

But men are not destined to fail in the battle for sexual purity. Victory is attainable, through the grace and power of God. But to achieve this, men need men—holding each other accountable, help-ing each other along, keeping one another true to God day by day.

KEY PRINCIPLE

If men are to be be sexually pure, they must have a network of oth-ers (including their spouses) who will hold them accountable and will call them to remain faithful and true to God.

KEY VERSE

"Therefore confess your sins to each other and pray for each other so that you may be healed. The prayer of a righteous man is powerful and effective" (James 5:16).

DISCUSSION QUESTIONS

1. Who is holding you accountable in this area of your life? How has this helped you with your sexual struggles? What do you

find most difficult about being held accountable? If no one is doing this in your life, whom could you ask to do so?

2. Whom do you hold accountable? How has this helped those men in their sexual struggles? How has this helped you? What do you find most difficult about holding other men accountable to be sexually pure?

3. Do you believe wives should hold their husbands accountable in this area? Does your wife hold you accountable? If not, why not? Have you revealed your struggles to your wife? If not, why not? What can you do today or in the near future to allow your wife a greater role in your quest for sexual purity?

CHAPTER FIFTEEN

What About Masturbation?

As men battle sexual lust, they sometimes give in to temptation by masturbating. Archibald Hart in his book *The Sexual Man* says, ". . . 95 percent (of men) started masturbating in their youth or early adulthood. . . . More than three out of four (77 percent) of them masturbate more than five times a month, and some as frequently as twice a day." Most of the books I have read see this as a normal practice that most men grow out of. However, Dr. Hart claims that 61 percent of all *married* men surveyed masturbate. The majority of these men, 82 percent, masturbate two to five times per month. "About 10 percent reported an average of between five and ten times per month; 6 percent reported more than fifteen times a month. A very small percentage, about 1 percent, report masturbating more than twenty times a month." When asked how married men feel about their masturbation, "almost all (97 percent) said they did not feel guilty. Only 2 percent said that it was shameful, and 8 percent that it was abnormal. But on the other hand, only 13 percent said they felt normal about masturbation. So what does this mean?

Either they genuinely don't know how they feel or they have a lot of ambivalence about their feelings. On the one hand, 97 percent said they don't feel guilty, but only 13 percent said it felt normal. . . . Gone are the days when men agonized over their masturbation."

I think these results show that a rationalization has taken place in our society. Men don't normally feel right about masturbation. Issues of self-control and conscience come into play, as does Jesus' admonition, "Anyone who looks at a woman lustfully has already committed adultery with her in his heart" (Matthew 5:28). Many of the married men I have spoken with agonize over their lack of self-control and self-discipline. They desire sex with their wives more often, but their wives don't have the same level of sexual desire for their husbands. Instead of facing rejection from their wives, the husbands masturbate. Based on Hart's research and my personal observations, I would have to say that most men do not grow out of the habit of masturbation. Marriage helps somewhat, but most men continue their adolescent practice of masturbation.

Our Lord calls all believers to be led and controlled by the Holy Spirit. Galatians 5:16-18, 22-23 says, "So I say, *live by the Spirit, and you will not gratify the desires of the sinful nature.* For the sinful nature desires what is contrary to the Spirit, and the Spirit what is contrary to the sinful nature. They are in conflict with each other, so that you do not do what you want. But if you are led by the Spirit, you are not under law. . . . But the fruit of the Spirit is love, joy, peace, patience, kindness, goodness, faithfulness, gentleness and *self-control.* Against such things there is no law" (emphasis mine). Spirit-controlled men don't masturbate! When we give in to this habit, we are walking in the flesh, not in the Spirit.

Men have as many reasons for masturbation as they do for sex. Many engage in the habit for emotional reasons—they are sad, glad, mad, angry, insecure, or fearful. Masturbation releases inner tension. However, if to accomplish this a man has to conjure up lustful thoughts or use pornography as a form of stimulation, it cannot be a holy act.

First Corinthians 6:12 says, "'Everything is permissible for me'—but not everything is beneficial. 'Everything is permissible for me'—but I will not be mastered by anything." Scripture clearly teaches that a follower of Jesus Christ is to not be dominated or controlled by anything or anyone except Jesus and His Spirit. Make no mistake about it—the habit of masturbation is addictive and controlling. Like gambling, overeating, drug and alcohol use, giving in repeatedly to this practice causes one to be under its control.

Romans 6:16 tells us, "Don't you know that when you offer yourselves to someone to obey him as slaves, you are slaves to the one whom you obey—whether you are slaves to sin, which leads to death, or to obedience, which leads to righteousness?" God wants to be God in every area of our lives. He wants to be our refuge when we need emotional relief. When we are stressed, He wants us to cast our anxieties onto Him (1 Peter 5:7), not go into a corner of some bathroom and masturbate.

We men sometimes tell ourselves that we just have to have a sexual release. But the fact is, thanks to the way God made us, if we have not had a sexual release for a period of time, our bodies will naturally release the excess semen. Physically, men are not harmed by not having sexual release.

One of the toughest battles Christian men face is that of controlling every thought for Christ. Second Corinthians 10:5 says, "We take captive every thought to make it obedient to Christ." We must grab every impure thought and bring it immediately into obedience to Christ. This again is where Scripture memorization under the control of the Holy Spirit is invaluable. You can be doing very well in the area of trying to stay pure, when an impure thought suddenly comes into your mind. Within seconds a choice must be made: fight the impure thought, or give in to it. Within seconds you may conclude, "I can't resist this" and decide you are going to masturbate. But the belief, however momentary, that the temptation is irresistible is a lie. Ephesians 4:22-24 says, "You were taught . . . to put off your old self, which is being corrupted by its deceitful desires; to be made new in the attitude of your minds; and . . . put on the new self, created to be like God in true righteousness and holiness."

One lie of the enemy is that you have no choice. Once you are thinking impure thoughts, have an erection, etc., you think you must masturbate. Not true. You always have a choice. Call out to God, and ask the Holy Spirit to control you. Romans 8:13 is true: "If by the Spirit you put to death the misdeeds of the body, you will live." So is 1 Corinthians 10:13, "No temptation has seized you except what is common to man. And God is faithful; he will not let you be tempted beyond what you can bear. But when you are tempted, he will also provide a way out so that you can stand up under it."

Let me conclude this chapter with the true story of a man I will call Bill. When my wife and I moved to Alameda, California, to minister to the sailors stationed there, we met Bill and his sister. Bill was an elderly gentleman close to ninety years old.

Almost every day I watched Bill shuffle down the street on his way to a local market. I thought to myself, "I had better share the Gospel with Bill soon. He may not have much longer to live."

I began planning my days so I could walk with Bill and start getting to know him. Several months later Bill didn't show up for his daily walk, so I went to his house and asked about him. His sister told me Bill had fallen at home and was in a nursing home. Several days later I went to visit Bill. In my pocket was a Gospel tract I wanted to share with him.

Bill was really glad to see me, but he looked horrible. His face had three to four days' growth of gray whiskers. His hair was uncombed. He told me he hated the food, disliked some of the other residents of the nursing home, and really wanted to go home. When I asked if I could share the Gospel, he agreed to listen. After I had gone through "The Four Spiritual Laws," I asked him if he had ever prayed to receive Christ. Bill started crying. After sobbing for several minutes, he mumbled something I couldn't quite understand. I asked him to repeat what he had said. After about four tries, as he sobbed I understood him to say, "Jesus could never forgive me."

I sat bewildered for several more minutes. I finally asked Bill, "What have you done that Jesus cannot forgive?" I was wondering if he'd been an ax murderer or a Nazi death camp guard or had committed some other horrible, seemingly unforgivable sin.

Several more minutes of weeping passed before Bill told me, "When I was a young man, I abused myself . . . and not just once. Four or five times I abused myself. I am so ashamed . . . God could never let me into His kingdom."

I knew from conversations with other men from his generation that the phrase "to abuse oneself" meant masturbation. I felt mad inside. Mad at Satan for his evil deception. Satan had tempted him, Bill had sinned, and Satan had kept him in guilt for over seventy years!

I explained to Bill that God could indeed forgive him. I showed him 1 John 1:9 and asked him to read it: "If we confess our sins, he is faithful and just and will forgive us our sins and purify us from all unrighteousness." He read it over and over again. At first he said God wouldn't forgive him. I assured Bill that God loved him. I asked Bill to memorize the verse on the spot. Between tears and sobs, after about ten minutes of working on it, Bill could quote it to me. His tears changed from hopeless tears to tears of joy. And he prayed with me to receive Christ, assured that God would indeed forgive him.

Oh, the riches of the promises of God! Second Peter 1:3-4 says, "His divine power has given us everything we need for life and godliness through our knowledge of him who called us by his own glory and goodness. Through these *he has given us his very great and precious promises*, so that through them you may participate in the divine nature and escape the corruption in the world caused by evil desires" (emphasis mine). The promises of God come to our rescue! Jesus said, "You will know the truth, and the truth will set you free" (John 8:32).

Bill was set free! You too can be liberated from guilt and bondage to sin through the magnificent promises and mercies of God.

We can experience and enjoy victory in our lives—victory through the power of the Holy Spirit as we choose to obey God. We do not have to keep yielding our bodies to impurity and to addictive iniquity. God is able to fill us, control us, and mold us so that we become men who please Him in every area of our lives.

KEY PRINCIPLE

We can say no to masturbation, an immoral means of relieving emotional tension and acting out sexual desires, only as we allow the Holy Spirit to be in control in our lives and mold our character.

KEY VERSES

"So I say, live by the Spirit, and you will not gratify the desires of the sinful nature. For the sinful nature desires what is contrary to the Spirit, and the Spirit what is contrary to the sinful nature. They are in conflict with each other, so that you do not do what you want. But if you are led by the Spirit, you are not under law. . . . But the fruit of the Spirit is love, joy, peace, patience, kindness, goodness, faithfulness, gentleness and self-control. Against such things there is no law" (Galatians 5:16-18, 22-23).

DISCUSSION QUESTIONS

1. Do you struggle with masturbation? Why or why not? Do you believe you can experience victory over this habit? Why or why not? What can you do today to let God help you? What human means might He use to bring this about?

2. Do you agree with the author that "Spirit-controlled men don't masturbate"? Why or why not? Why would God not want Christian men to act out their sexual desires in this way?

3. When you masturbate, how does that affect your feelings about yourself? God? Your wife? When you are tempted but say no to the temptation, how do you feel about yourself? God? Your wife? Why is this?

CHAPTER SIXTEEN

Drunk
or Filled?

Joe was new at the job. When his boss asked him to go out for a drink after work, he was excited. He looked forward to being accepted, and maybe even scoring some points with his boss. Even though he was well aware of the dangers of alcohol, he felt he could risk a few drinks for the sake of his career. After several glasses, he began to talk freely and "enjoy" himself. He ordered several more drinks. Things kind of blacked out after that. He couldn't remember when one of the women in the bar joined their group or when she suggested they retire to his apartment. When he woke up the next morning, he was shocked to find a woman lying naked in his bed. He had no idea who she was or how she got there. Joe was gripped with fear. What had he done? What would his boss think? What if he'd contracted some deadly disease?

This fictitious account unfortunately plays itself out every day across our nation. Alcohol and drugs dull the senses and lower the inhibitions. The strongest convictions begin to crumble as booze enters a man's body.

Is it wrong to drink alcoholic beverages? Though there are no prohibitions on drinking alcohol, the Scriptures do clearly teach that it's wrong to get drunk. Ephesians 5:18 says, "Do not get drunk on wine, which leads to debauchery. Instead, be filled with the Spirit." Drunkenness is always associated with the deeds of the flesh—our old nature, what we were before we came to know Jesus Christ as our personal Savior. Galatians 5:19-21 says, "The acts of the sinful nature are obvious: *sexual immorality*, impurity and debauchery . . . factions and envy; *drunkenness*, orgies, and the like" (emphasis mine). It is no surprise that excessive consumption of alcohol and sexual impurity are linked together. The experience of many has proven the connection. Since liquor lowers one's ability to resist fleshly sins, a man striving for a sexually pure life will be wise to avoid the influence of alcohol.

Two Old Testament saints, both mentioned in the New Testament, sadly illustrate the connection between sexual sin and drunkenness. Noah is mentioned in the "Hall of Faith" (Hebrews 11:7). Lot, Abraham's nephew, was mentioned by Jesus (Luke 17:28-29) and by Peter (2 Peter 2:7-8). Their godly faith is worth imitating. However, an event from each man's life is recorded that is *not* worth following.

Lot traveled with Abraham to the promised land from Ur of the Chaldeans, and God prospered both of them. As their flocks grew, Abraham and Lot eventually went separate ways to avoid conflict between their servants over water rights from the scarce wells. Lot chose first and picked the lush, green valley where the towns of Sodom and Gomorrah were. What Lot saw happening in those towns was disgusting to him. Second Peter 2:7-9 says:

. . . if he rescued Lot, a righteous man, who was distressed by the filthy lives of lawless men (for that righteous man, living among them day after day, was tormented in his righteous soul by the lawless deeds he saw and heard)—if this is so, then the Lord knows how to rescue godly men from trials and to hold the unrighteous for the day of judgment, while continuing their punishment.

When the wicked cries of Sodom and Gomorrah reached God's ears, He sent destroying angels down to destroy those cities. Genesis 19 describes the scene. Because of the powerful prayer of Abraham, Lot and his immediate family were rescued by angels who "grasped his hand and the hands of his wife and of his two daughters and led them safely out of the city, for the LORD was merciful to them. As soon as they had brought them out, one of them said, 'Flee for your lives! Don't look back'" (verses 16-17). Lot's wife refused to obey, looked back, and became a pillar of salt (verse 26). We pick up the story again in verses 30-36.

Lot and his two daughters left Zoar and settled in the mountains, for he was afraid to stay in Zoar. He and his two daughters lived in a cave. One day the older daughter said to the younger, "Our father is old, and there is no man around here to lie with us, as is the custom all over the earth. Let's get our father to drink wine and then lie with him and preserve our family line through our father." That night they got their father to drink wine, and the older daughter went in and lay with him. He was not aware of it when she lay down or when she got up. The next day the older daughter said to the younger, "Last night I lay with my father. Let's get him to drink wine again tonight, and you go in and lie with him so we can preserve our family line through our father." So they got their father to drink wine

*that night also, and the younger daughter went and lay with
him. Again he was not aware of it when she lay down or
when she got up. So both of Lot's daughters became pregnant by their father.*

Lot's daughters clearly knew that what they were doing was
wrong. They used wine to get their righteous father to sin sexually. If Lot had known that drinking wine would lead to his committing incest, do you think he would have taken that first drink?
Alcohol is often used to get someone to sin sexually in our day as
well.

Noah is one of my heroes of faith. God told Noah to build a
ship because He intended to destroy sinful mankind except for
righteous Noah and his family. For over 100 years Noah labored
with his sons, cutting down trees and building the huge boat. All
the while, the people mocked him, but faithful Noah kept building—even though it had never rained before on the earth! What
amazing faith!

The floods came as predicted, and Noah and his family were
the sole survivors. When the ark landed, Noah planted himself a
vineyard. I don't know why, but he decided to make himself some
wine. Maybe he felt entitled to a drink after so many years of
hardship and strenuous work. Maybe he wanted to escape some
of the awful memories of the Flood, the deaths of his former
friends and and indeed of all mankind. Maybe he feared the future
or was tired of always having to be good.

We pick up the story in Genesis 9:20-25:

*Noah, a man of the soil, proceeded to plant a vineyard.
When he drank some of its wine, he became drunk and lay
uncovered inside his tent. Ham, the father of Canaan, saw*

his father's nakedness and told his two brothers outside. But
Shem and Japheth took a garment and laid it across their
shoulders; then they walked in backward and covered their
father's nakedness. Their faces were turned the other way so
that they would not see their father's nakedness. When Noah
awoke from his wine and found out what his youngest son
had done to him, he said, "Cursed be Canaan! The lowest
of slaves will he be to his brothers."

The first recorded sin after the Flood had to do with nakedness, and the root cause of this was drunkenness. This is the only negative event recorded in Scripture about Noah, one weak moment when he decided to drink wine and lay uncovered in his tent.

In all fairness to Noah, we don't know for sure that he knew he would get drunk from drinking the juice of the grapes. After the Flood the earth was a different place than before, and it is possible, some scholars believe, that this was the first time of wine fermentation. We also don't exactly know what sin Ham committed. The text does show, however, that both of the other brothers were careful not to look upon Noah's nakedness, even walking backwards to avoid seeing him. Where was Noah's wife during this drunken episode? Was she also naked with Noah? Many questions cannot be fully answered.

First Peter 5:8 says, "Be self-controlled and alert. Your enemy the devil prowls around like a roaring lion looking for someone to devour." In the battle against sexual temptation, we must always be on guard. As a believer, if you decide to use your freedom to drink alcoholic beverages, remember that you thus increase your vulnerability to sin in the area of sexual purity.

KEY PRINCIPLE

Excessive consumption of alcoholic beverages makes men vulnerable to sexual immorality and is not part of the Spirit-filled life God desires for them.

KEY VERSE

"Do not get drunk on wine, which leads to debauchery. Instead, be filled with the Spirit" (Ephesians 5:18).

DISCUSSION QUESTIONS

1. Where do you stand on the issue of drinking alcohol as a believer? Why? Have you personally studied the key Scriptures that discuss this issue?

2. If you have ever consumed alcohol excessively, what was the most costly thing you did as a result (in terms of consequences, not dollars)? How would things have been different if you had been filled with the Spirit instead of being drunk?

3. What safeguards can you take to prevent committing sexual sin if you drink alcoholic beverages, even in moderation? If you are married, discuss all this with your wife, and be willing to listen to her point of view. Are you willing to be held accountable by your spouse and/or by a close Christian friend or spiritual leader?

CHAPTER SEVENTEEN

Smart Bombs and Cybersex

I watched my TV in amazement as the Pentagon spokesman explained what was happening. An Iraqi building was getting closer and closer, looming larger and larger. We were seeing what the smart bomb was seeing. The bomb had been dropped from an American warplane and was being guided by a combination of laser beams from another airplane and the smart bomb's own guidance system. The precise target was a two-foot-square ventilation duct. With uncanny accuracy, the smart bomb did what it was designed to do, penetrating the center of the duct and entering the building. Seconds later, the building shook, then collapsed.

The Pentagon spokesman clicked the controls, and another Iraqi building came into view. The same scenario took place. Different target, different bomb, same result. Over and over again, smart bombs were doing exactly what they were designed to do—travel over long distances and destroy the exact building targeted, with minimal risk to the pilots.

Some of the same technology used in the development of smart bombs is available to civilians through personal computers.

Computers at work and home are revolutionizing the way we live. From balancing checkbooks to desktop publishing to educational games, almost every aspect of our lives can be related in some way to computer capabilities. Computers even talk to each other through modems. I can create a document on my computer and transmit it to another computer thousands of miles away. Incredible!

The information superhighway is a vast, electronic system connecting millions of computers around the world. Originally designed for use within governmental agencies, educational institutions, and the military, it now services the private sector. Commercial companies like CompuServe, America Online, and Prodigy allow their subscribers to access the Internet. A subscriber can connect to millions of different services in almost any country of the world. The amount of information available is staggering.

Even though this technology is a tremendous blessing, the immoral use of it is a curse. Sinful humans, seduced by the prince of the power of the air and enticed by a profit motive, have flooded the Internet with pornography. Helpful information is easy to obtain via the computer, but so is explicit sexual stimulation. This is cybersex—sex via the computer.

Pornography used to be available only in certain "red light" districts of large cities. With the relaxing of obscenity laws, these sex businesses widened their reach. Thanks to VCR's, men began to rent pornographic movies and bring them into their own homes. With the further advance of cable TV and satellite technology, smut can now be beamed directly into a man's living room. With the further advance of computers and modems, sexual sin is more private and hidden than ever.

Just as superior American war technology overwhelmed the Iraqis, Satan, promoting lust and sexual license, has used advanced technology to destroy many men in the privacy of their own homes or workplaces. If men do not guard their souls as they navigate the Internet, they will be destroyed by high-tech pornography. To lust over seductive images on a computer screen leads to spiritual disaster. As James 1:13-16 says, "When tempted, no one should say, 'God is tempting me.' For God cannot be tempted by evil, nor does he tempt anyone; but each one is tempted when, by his own evil desire, he is dragged away and enticed. Then, *after desire has conceived, it gives birth to sin; and sin, when it is fullgrown, gives birth to death.* Don't be deceived, my dear brothers" (emphasis mine). Pornography on the Internet has already caused numerous Christian men to stumble and will undoubtedly cause many more to fall. We must beware.

I know four Christian men who have stumbled through the use of cybersex in the past year alone. I want to share the testimony of one of them, a friend of mine who wanted to share his struggles with others. We can all learn from this brother's experience, which he describes in his own written account below.

THE TESTIMONY
OF A CYBERSEX CASUALTY

Computer online sex is an issue for many Christian brothers. I humbly share my experience to help readers understand the vulnerability we all have to the way Satan uses new technologies to entrap men trying to serve God.

I had been a subscriber to a popular computer online service for about six weeks when I saw an announcement to try out the "romance connection" chat rooms. I thought to myself, "Why not?" I clicked the appropriate icon, and there I was in the midst of a room with twenty-three other people all looking for someone to "pick up on" for a private (or perhaps group) cybersex session. I scrolled through the screen names of several participants, picked out one that resembled a female name, and sent an instant message: "Hi there. What are you up to?" She quickly replied back, "Hi!" Soon I was engrossed in a conversation about our personal sex lives. Then I asked her, "Would you like to dance?" She said, "Of course, but you lead."

For the next twenty minutes we led each other through a fantasy date that ended up with our having sex on the dance floor. I certainly felt guilty, but what made this experience seem "safe" was that nobody would know about it. It provided a greater rush than viewing pornography because it involved the human interaction of two willing individuals.

After that experience I learned how to attach a personal profile to my online name. Actually, I developed a pseudo-name and even fake profile information. I didn't indicate that I was married (later I found it didn't matter to online partners if I was married or not), understated my weight, overstated my height, and generally embellished my profile.

My first experience with cybersex lasted for a period of about three or four days. I was possessed with a passion for the computer, spent two or three hours at a sitting, and had cybersex with over ten different women. After those days the newness of the experience wore off, and it seemed as if I gotten it out of my system. I confessed my sin to God and prayed for a cleansed heart. He was faithful to forgive me, and I lost interest in the matter for about a month. I stayed away from the chat rooms and refrained from using the online service except for the e-mail feature.

Then one day I thought I ought to erase my pseudo-name. I

erased the pseudo-name, but rather than signing off, I succumbed to an even more vile temptation. I created a female name and pro-file, logged on as a woman, went to the various chat rooms, and found myself inundated with Instant Messages from horny male sub-scribers. Out of curiosity, I went along with them. Some were very upfront and graphic about having cybersex; others were more sub-tle and polite. After that session I became very disgusted with myself. Shame and guilt filled my heart. Not only over the sin I had committed against God and my wife, but because I felt bad for all the other people who were affected. I was amazed at the widespread interest in having cybersex. A few days later I deleted my female name and profile and again had victory over temptations for a few weeks.

Then once again I fell into the trap. I spent several hours one night flirting online with females. I even had one agree to fly to my town and meet me at a hotel for a day. She was eager to do so. Fortunately, fantasy came too close to reality for me, and I felt so empty over the matter that I completely erased all pseudo-names and found refuge in Christ. I sought counsel and account-ability from some Christian men whom I trusted. Moreover, I gained help by meditating on Scripture. For the past several months I have had victory over my sinful online service uses and am confident that God is able to deliver me from these tempta-tions.

What helped me most to remain pure was to understand and deal with some of the root causes of my temptation. Obviously I'd committed adultery in my heart. I needed to confess that as sin, but I also discovered that I had violated the first two of the Ten Commandments. I had set up false gods and idols in my life. When I identified the false gods, repented (volitionally turning away from them), and confessed it as sin, God brought full victory. Online computer sex had become an idol of pleasure. I'd sought sexual gratification by a method not designed by God. God instituted marriage as a holy, pure means for mutual sexual satisfaction. God's plan is for me to seek to please my wife; Satan's plan is for me to seek self-gratification from others besides my wife. The battle for me is to discipline myself to postpone instant gratification for future rewards.

I praise God that I am working toward consistent victory in my thought life. I have such freedom now to turn on my computer and use it for the glory of God and not for my flesh!

I hope this brother's testimony helps you in some way.

Even thought this is all relatively new technology, we must not be ignorant of the spiritual threats it presents. Second Corinthians 2:11 says, ". . . in order that Satan might not outwit us. For we are not unaware of his schemes." We must be on our guard—the prince of the power of the air, using high-tech weaponry, has infiltrated cyberspace. Every computer that has a modem is susceptible. If you regularly use a computer, you may have already been tempted, or maybe you already have a secret life. Numbers 32:23 says, "You may be sure that your sin will find you out." Though in the original context, this refers to the sin of not doing as we have promised (to defend our brothers in battle), the principle is clear: no sin is hidden or secret or without consequences. God sees what we are doing, and our sin will affect ourselves and those around us.

If you must use the Internet, use it with caution. Stay away from sexually oriented chat rooms. If you have struggled with cybersex, confess your failings to another brother, your wife, or a support group. Don't let your children surf the net unsupervised.

Reader's Digest recently reported a story of how child pornographers and molesters are using the net to find new victims. The same principles you must use to keep from sinning sexually with your TV and VCR apply to the computer. Develop a purity plan, and use it whenever you use your computer. Don't give in to curiosity and go exploring for sexually explicit material. Some software programs block your computer from accessing such material. The problem is, these programs become outdated very quickly since pornographers keep devising new programs and marketing tools to push their products.

According to a recent *Focus on the Family* radio program, pornography is an *eight billion dollar a year industry*. With such a lucrative market, sinful men will do anything they can to entice others to look at their smut. Pornographers have human, fleshly nature on their side. As Proverbs 27:20 says, "Death and Destruction are never satisfied, and neither are the eyes of man." There will always be a market for pornography.

The issue for the Christian man is, will you be smart and godly and resist the temptation, with God's help, or will you be naive and fall?

KEY PRINCIPLE

Men today must beware of cybersex—sexual stimulation through pornography and immoral chat rooms on the Internet.

KEY VERSES

"When tempted, no one should say, 'God is tempting me.' For God cannot be tempted by evil, nor does he tempt anyone; but

each one is tempted when, by his own evil desire, he is dragged away and enticed. Then, after desire has conceived, it gives birth to sin; and sin, when it is full-grown, gives birth to death. Don't be deceived, my dear brothers" (James 1:13-16).

DISCUSSION QUESTIONS

1. If you own a computer and modem, do you struggle with cybersex temptations? What are the causes for this? Are you fighting back, or are you a willing victim?

2. Have you told another brother or your spouse or whoever about your struggles? Why or why not? What benefits do you foresee in someone else's knowing? What drawbacks? Would it be worth the risk?

3. What can you do to keep from being a casualty to this sin? Be practical and be specific. If you have already fallen, what can you do to minimize the damage or to restore what has been lost, if possible? Where does God fit into the picture?

Down
But Not Out

The first torpedo stuck on the port side between frames 46 and 60. Soon after that, the second torpedo struck on the same side between frames 95 and 100, below the armor belt. The blasts opened huge holes, allowing tons of seawater to enter the wounded ship. Then the dive bombers came, scoring one direct hit. Another bomb dropped close by, causing further damage. Flooding occurred through open manholes, ventilation systems, and ruptured pipelines. Three days later the ship finally sank where it was berthed, alongside Ford Island, where other ships hit in the attack were in the process of sinking or had already sunk. The USS *California* joined the USS *West Virginia*, the USS *Oglala*, the USS *Downes*, the USS *Cassin*, the USS *Nevada*, the USS *Arizona*, and the USS *Shaw*—all of them attacked at Pearl Harbor on December 7, 1941.

But the story does not end there. After a ship is sunk, it is not necessarily lost forever. It may be useless in the short run but not long-term. Foresighted leaders knew the war would be a long one, and that given time, even sunken ships, if salvaged properly, could be useful in the war effort. So the long process of resurrecting useless, broken, flooded, and burned-out ships began.

The first priority after an attack is to prepare for another one. There was a very real chance that the Japanese would return to finish the job they had started. Gun mounts had to be manned continuously, ammunition replenished, preparations made for a possible landing of Japanese troops. All of these preparations would take able-bodied laborers away from the process of restoring broken ships to usefulness. Many historians believe the real Japanese failure at Pearl Harbor was that they did not return.

The next priority, occurring simultaneously with the first, is to save lives. Fires must be extinguished, flooding stopped or at least controlled where possible. Men who jumped overboard to escape burning ships have to be fished out of the water. Next comes the rescuing of men trapped in the sunken ships, saved by drilling holes in the hulls of the overturned vessels.

How did the American Navy refloat the ships that were sunk, then make them usable again? First, the holes letting the water into the hull were plugged. Then large pumps were brought on board the ship to remove water trapped inside the vessel. When enough buoyancy was created, the ships floated themselves. Next followed the removal of all the supplies, oil and fuel, and ammunition, lightening the ships of all unnecessary weight. Then came the removal of bodies. In the dewatering process, two feet of water was left on the deck, and the bodies were then floated into large canvas bags to be transported to a naval hospital for identification and burial.

Next, all equipment damaged by the saltwater was removed. After that, each compartment was washed down with saltwater, then washed with a hot caustic solution to remove the oil residue from the walls and floors, followed by a freshwater washdown. Temporary ventilation had to be installed, and temporary lights as well. Because hazardous gases were a danger, every compartment that had been flooded had to be tested before allowing anyone to enter. Each piece of equipment had to be dried out, checked for operability, then reinstalled.

On March 24th, 1942, 107 days after being sunk, the USS *California* was brought to the surface. After six months of makeshift repairs in Pearl Harbor, it steamed under its own power to Puget Sound Naval Shipyard in Bremerton, Washington. For another year thousands of men and women worked to restore the mighty ship to its former fighting capabilities. Late in 1943 the USS *California* rejoined the Pacific Fleet and fought in Saipan. Later it participated in the bombardment of Guam. Then on October 25, 1944, she fought in the Battle of Surigao Strait. In that battle the USS *California* pumped over 1,500 projectiles into a large Japanese battleship.

By the time World War II had ended, the USS *California* had won seven battle stars against the Japanese forces. Not bad for a ship that once lay full of seawater and dead bodies on the bottom of Pearl Harbor.

When torpedoes of temptation explode within you, bombs of lustful thinking, flames of passion and sexual sin, you may have lost the battle. You may be on fire, listing severely, and taking on water. You may have abandoned ship and lost all hope of ever being pure, of ever being useful to the Master who created and designed you. You may have even knowingly scuttled yourself by giving up in the battle for sexual purity. But the Master is not done with you. Just as the USS *California* lay useless on the bottom of the ocean, you may be useless in your current state, but you're not out of the war permanently. There is hope. God is a salvage expert. He knows how to make broken ships useful again. He can fix broken bodies and useless believers and make them whole again.

It is a long war, and there are numerous battles. The USS *California* could have been sunk in a later battle, but it wasn't. She contributed to the overall war effort, functioned according to her design, and helped win the war. She was credited with ribbons for her efforts. If we allow the Master to resurrect us, to give us a fresh start, first in salvation, then in restoration, we can help win the war. We too can win crowns for our efforts.

Don't give up! You can be refloated. Your hull can be patched. Fires can be put out, useless equipment replaced. You may have scars that can't be changed, but as you receive divine strength you can again enter the battle and live a holy life. Psalm 3:5 says, "I wake again, because the LORD sustains me." As long as you have breath, the Lord is not finished with you. Lamentations 3:22-23 says, "Because of the LORD's great love we are not consumed, for his compassions never fail. They are new every morning; great is your faithfulness."

The story of Samson (Judges 13—16) is a wonderful account of losing the battle to lust but regaining usefulness at the hands of a merciful, forgiving God. Chosen by God to be a judge or deliverer of Israel, to fight and defeat the Philistine oppressors, Samson had a special calling—that of a Nazirite. As part of this special mission, he was never to touch a dead body, never to consume wine, never to cut his hair—a symbol of his unique heaven-sent role. But little by little Samson compromised his calling, leading to a dramatic downfall. Finally, because of Delilah's persistent nagging, Samson revealed to her the secret of his strength, and when the locks of his hair fell onto Delilah's lap, his strength fell with them. When Samson woke up, he was ignorant of his helplessness. The Philistines then grabbed him, tied him up, and gouged out his eyes as he shrieked in pain. Cheers from the Philistines drowned out the broken, whimpering cries of God's defeated champion.

Samson's reason and judgment had been blinded by lust. He had been sleeping with the enemy but failed to realize the danger to his own soul and to his people. Delilah used her fleshly charms to seduce him, and he fell into sexual sin. Broken, blinded, and being used for sport, Samson was a pitiful sight. But in time his hair began to grow back, and his strength started to return. Then one day the Philistines brought Samson out into an arena to mock him. The Philistine god Dagon was being worshiped, and a man God had chosen as a special vessel was being humiliated. Samson prayed for strength one last time, and God saw Samson's brokenness, his helplessness, and the plight of Israel. Jealous because a false god was being given the worship due only to Himself, God granted Samson's request, again giving him supernatural strength. Samson died in the process but killed more Philistines in his death than in his life.

God used blind Samson for His glory. Even though Samson was scarred, he was still usable. He never regained his physical sight, but he did recover his spiritual sight and called on God to help him do what he had been designed to do in the first place—deliver Israel from Philistine domination.

An alarming number of adults in America have had or currently have a sexually transmitted disease, some of these incurable. Many women are sterile at the hands of lying, diseased men who lied just to obtain sexual pleasure. Many men suffer from the guilt of moral failure and are afraid they will be exposed and suffer job loss and social rejection. Others fear their wives will leave them if their secret sexual sin is found out. Some fear jail or imprisonment for crimes they have committed because of their failure to tame their sex drive. Sadly, many of these men are Christians. Sadder yet, many of these believers do not believe that God can or will forgive them. Seeing themselves as beyond recovery because of their out-of-control sex drive, they have lost hope that they can ever live righteous lives.

I have good news for you. The God who gave Samson back his strength is the same God who wants to forgive and heal you. You may have lost the battle; in fact, you may have lost lots of battles. You may be in the enemy camp right now, a prisoner of war, just like Samson; but God can set you free. Repent, acknowledge any sinful actions and attitudes, and seek God's grace. God longs to heal you, to restore you, to put you back on the path of holy living and joyful, productive service. God longs to use you to rescue the souls of men. Isaiah 55:6-9 tells us, "Seek the LORD while he may be found; call on him while he is near. Let the wicked forsake his way and the evil man his thoughts. Let him turn to the LORD, and he will have mercy on him, and to our God, for he will freely pardon. 'For my thoughts are not your thoughts, neither are your ways my ways,' declares the LORD. 'As the heavens are higher than the earth, so are my ways higher than your ways and my thoughts than your thoughts.'" *There is no sexual sin that God cannot forgive.*

You may ask, "But what about my guilt? How do I know God will forgive me? Why don't I feel forgiven when I confess my sin?" It is imperative that we remember that the only basis for forgiveness is God's mercy, grace, and love. In Psalm 25:6-7 David said, "Remember, O LORD, your great mercy and love, for they are from old. Remember not the sins of my youth and my rebellious ways; according to your love remember me, for you are good, O LORD." Isaiah 43:25 adds, "I, even I, am he who blots out your transgressions, for my own sake, and remembers your sins no more." God desires our fellowship, but the only way He can fellowship with us is to blot out our sins and wipe us clean. Because He loves us, He desires a relationship with us. We don't deserve this, and we can't earn it. Friendship with God comes only by His grace. "The law was given through Moses; grace and truth came through Jesus Christ" (John 1:17).

Because of the finished work of Christ on the cross, we have access to God. Because of the substitutionary death of the Lord Jesus Christ, we have been forgiven once for all time. Because of Jesus we are destined to stand before God holy, spotless. and blameless. When we break fellowship with God by sinning, we do not lose our membership in the family of God but must simply obey 1 John 1:9 and confess or agree with God that we have sinned. The Lord then forgives us again, just as He promised.

As believers in Christ, we must refuse to mope at self-imposed pity parties of guilt. To wallow in our failure is to continue thinking about the very things the Lord has commanded us not to think about. Satan uses guilt and accusations to keep our focus on ourselves, our failures, and our sin rather than on God and on Christ through whose blood we have forgiveness. If Satan can keep us distracted in our focus, we will fall to sin again—perhaps in the very area we just confessed.

In the area of sexual sin, the guilt seems to be overwhelming. We must therefore all the more discipline our minds to think on the Lord, to reckon ourselves dead to sin, to resist the attacks of the enemy, and to believe the promises of God, knowing that He loves to restore and rebuild. With this hope, let us keep fighting the battle for sexual purity. "We are more than conquerors through him who loved us" (Romans 8:37).

> *Surely you desire truth in the inner parts; you teach me wisdom in the inmost place. Cleanse me with hyssop, and I will be clean; wash me, and I will be whiter than snow. Let me hear joy and gladness; let the bones you have crushed rejoice. Hide your face from my sins and blot out all my iniquity. Create in me a pure heart, O God, and renew a steadfast spirit within me. Do not cast me from your presence or take your Holy Spirit from me. Restore to me the joy of your salvation and grant me a willing spirit, to sustain me. Then I will teach transgressors your ways, and sinners will turn back to you.*
>
> *—Psalm 51:6-13*

KEY PRINCIPLE

No matter what moral failures we have suffered, no matter how hard we've fallen, God wants to forgive us and make us whole and useful and victorious.

KEY VERSES

"Because of the LORD's great love we are not consumed, for his compassions never fail. They are new every morning; great is your faithfulness" (Lamentations 3:22-23).

DISCUSSION QUESTIONS

1. Do you have a Christian brother you can confide in? If not, ask God to give you one with whom you can share your darkest, secret sin and who will affirm, challenge, and direct you in your spiritual walk.

2. Do you really believe in God's promise to forgive, cleanse, and restore (Psalm 51:6-13; 1 John 1:9)? Why or why not? How does this impact your daily life?

3. Do you believe that one day you will consistently walk in obedience and purity? If so, what is the basis for this confidence? What can you do today to work toward this goal? How does God fit into the picture?

A FINAL WORD

At the start of World War II, Hitler's strategy was twofold: submarines and the Luftwaffe (air force). Operating in groups called wolf packs, his submarines sank thousands of Allied ships, choking off the supply lines to Great Britain. At the same time, the German air force was bombing England and sinking ship convoys. The air and subsurface threats almost forced England to surrender. Though the Germans had a few surface warships in various ports at the start of the war, they needed more and so built several other major combatants. Two were completed about the same time—the *Prinz Eugen* and the *Bismarck*.

The *Bismarck* was the most formidable warship ever built up to that time. She had eight guns with barrels fifteen inches in diameter. These guns could fire at enemy ships over twenty-two miles away, lobbing shells weighing as much as a Volkswagen bug. In addition, she had over 16,000 tons of armor to protect herself. She was also designed with numerous watertight compartments to prevent flooding throughout the ship. The *Bismarck* was trouble for any warship that would challenge it.

The first naval encounter the *Bismarck* faced was against the equally formidable HMS *Hood*, the pride of the British Naval Fleet, a ship with a long history of honor and gallant service. In their first encounter, the *Bismarck* showed its superior firepower and accuracy. One of the large shells hit the *Hood* right in the middle, where there was a weak spot in the armor. The shell penetrated an ammunition magazine and exploded the entire magazine. The *Hood* broke into two pieces and sank in minutes, killing most of its crew. Shock waves rippled throughout the British and Allied fleets. Winston Churchill soon uttered his now-famous line, "Sink the *Bismarck*."

Now besides the threat of wolf packs and the aerial threat of German bombers, the Allies had to worry about the *Bismarck* and her escort, the *Prinz Eugen*. The war was now being fought above, below, and on the surface of the waters. The Allied commanders ordered every available asset to search for, find, and sink the *Bismarck*. This process took several weeks and involved hundreds of ships and planes—one of the most comprehensive, focused endeavors of the war. Once the Allies located the *Bismarck*, a fortunate torpedo hit damaged its rudder, making it virtually impossible for it to maneuver or to outrun the Allied attacks. Even once it was a sitting duck, it took hundreds of direct hits before the *Bismarck* was sunk. It took an all-out effort to remove the threat of that one ship. But by removing it, victory began to be won.

This picture from World War II shows what should and can be done with pornography and the whole illicit sex industry. Pornography presents a seemingly invincible danger to anyone desiring to walk in purity. In the early 1950s Hugh Hefner and others launched an immoral *Bismarck* on the world. Under the cover of First Amendment rights, thousands of men have fallen prey to the enemy's lures in *Playboy*, *Penthouse*, and other slick magazines. Lies such as "a victimless crime," "innocent pleasure," and "entertainment for men" have led thousands of men into addictive sexual practices and caused sexual dissatisfaction leading to thousands of divorces and child molestation cases. The only way to curb the sale of pornographic material is for offended citizens to rise up and elect public officials who share their moral beliefs. Elected officials then need to appoint judges with a strong moral background and character and prosecute pornographers to the fullest extent of the law.

Every Christian needs to urge store owners and shopkeepers not to sell profitable but pornographic magazines and videos. I saw a bumper sticker that said, "Stores That Sell Pornography Don't Sell Anything to Me." These magazines feed the flesh and expose successive generations of youth to the lies and myths of unfulfilling, immoral, and deadly sexual practices. Only with the Lord's help can we turn this nation back to honoring women as women and not as sex objects and to protecting our children from aberrant sexual behavior and philosophies. According to *Citizen* magazine (October 21, 1991), a ministry of Focus on the Family, more than sixty cities have rid themselves of pornography. For more information, write: National Coalition for the Protection of Children & Families, 800 Compton, Suite 9224, Cincinnati, OH 45234 or the National Family Legal Foundation, 3030 North Third Street, Suite 200, Phoenix, AZ 85012.

Have you ever taken a public stand against pornography? Do you feel the Lord might be calling you to speak out against this evil? If you feel the Lord is calling you to battle, remember his words to his servant Joshua: "Be strong and courageous. Do not

be terrified; do not be discouraged, for the LORD your God will
be with you wherever you go" (Joshua 1:9).

In our personal lives and in our society, with God's help, as
we faithfully and bravely serve our Lord Jesus Christ, we can
experience victory!

KEY PRINCIPLES AND VERSES: A SUMMARY

For a polluted mind—REMEMBER
Psalm 119:9, 11
*"How can a young man keep his way pure? By living according
to your word . . . . I have hidden your word in my heart that I
might not sin against you"*

When under demonic attack—RESIST
James 4:7-8
*"Submit yourselves, then, to God. Resist the devil, and he will flee
from you. Come near to God and he will come near to you. Wash
your hands, you sinners, and purify your hearts, you double-
minded."*

When under attack by a worldly environment—RETREAT
2 Timothy 2:22
*"In a large house there are articles not only of gold and silver,
but also of wood and clay; some are for noble purposes and
some for ignoble. If a man cleanses himself from the latter, he
will be an instrument for noble purposes, made holy, useful to the
Master amd prepared to do any good work. Flee the evil desires
of youth, and pursue righteousness, faith, love and peace, along
with those who call on the Lord out of a pure heart."*

When the flesh desires to sin—RECKON
Romans 6:10-13
"The death he [Christ] died, he died to sin once for all; but the life he lives, he lives to God. In the same way, count yourselves dead to sin but alive to God in Christ Jesus. Therefore do not let sin reign in your mortal body so that you obey its evil desires. Do not offer the parts of your body to sin, as instruments of wickedness, but rather offer youselves to God, as those who have been brought from death to life; and offer the parts of your body to him as instruments of righteousness."

When emotional needs are unmet—TAKE REFUGE
Psalm 62:8
"Trust in him at all times, O people; pour out your hearts to him, for God is our refuge."

BIBLIOGRAPHY

Billheimer, Paul. *Destined to Overcome*. Minneapolis: Bethany House, 1982.

Carnes, Patrick. *Out of the Shadows*. CompCare Publishers, 1987.

—— *Contrary to Love*. CompCare Publishers, 1989.

Caton, David E. *Pornography: The Addiction*. Tampa, Fla.: Canaan Ministry, 1989.

Cavendish, Marshall, editor. *Marshall Cavendish Illustrated Encyclopedia of World War II*, Volume 9, Chapter 4: "*Shinano*." n.p., 1985.

Colson, Charles. *Loving God*. Grand Rapids: Zondervan, 1987.

Farrar, Steve. *Point Man*. Portland: Multnomah, 1990.

Hart, Archibald D. *The Sexual Man*. Waco, Tex.: Word, 1994.

Hicks, Robert. *The Masculine Journey*. Colorado Springs: NavPress, 1991.

Morison, Samuel Eliot. *The Two Ocean War*. New York: Little, Brown and Company, 1963.

Swindoll, Charles. *Dropping Your Guard*. Waco, Tex.: Word, 1993.

Taylor, Theodore. *Battle in the Arctic Seas*, Chapter 8: "The Story of Convoy PQ 17." New York: Thomas Y. Crowell, 1976.

Wallin, Homer N. *Pearl Harbor: Why, How, Fleet Salvage and Final Appraisal*, Chapter 3. Washington, D.C.: Naval History Division, United States Navy, 1968.

A PRAYER

Dear heavenly Father,
Please challenge and encourage and equip each person who has read this book. Please help him apply to his life the principles You have shown him. Where you have convicted of sin, please grant the grace to repent. Where there needs to be reconciliation, please give the boldness to take the initiative so healing can occur. Where action needs to be taken, please give the strength to obey. If some are barely hanging on, please grant needed strength. Where there is blindness due to lust, please open eyes and hearts. In relationships where forgiveness needs to be given, please give the ability to forgive, as Christ has forgiven us.

O most merciful Father, please bestow mercy on our sinful nation. We as a people are calling wrong right. We mask the true nature of our sexual sins against You and against each other. We exalt nakedness and immorality and then wonder why there is rampant disease and illegitimacy and broken relationships and alienation and overwhelming sadness. We have elected officials to lead us who are immoral and who appoint ungodly judges to determine right from wrong. We have passed laws making it difficult to prosecute those who prey sexually on our young.

Father, may Your Holy Spirit descend upon us, convicting us of our sin. Please lead Your people to repentance and brokenness so we can again be Your pure people. Help us to hear and heed Your voice.

Father, we need You. Please open our eyes so we as a people will repent, turn from our wicked ways, and seek Your face. Father, please heal our land. Forgive us for our willing failures; strengthen us for battle; equip us for victory; set our eyes upon Jesus and His perseverance, our only hope for change and conquest over sexual impurity. In the name of our Lord and Savior, Jesus Christ,

Amen.

God: Psalm 62:8; Isaiah 6:3; Lamentations 3:22-23; 1 Peter 1:15-16.

Habits: Romans 6:17-18; Ephesians 4:22-24; Ephesians 5:18.

Helping Each Other: Ecclesiastes 4:9-10, 12; Hebrews 3:13.

Hope: Psalm 3:5; Philippians 1:6.

Jesus: Hebrews 2:18; 1 John 3:2-3.

Marriage: Proverbs 5:15-19; 1 Corinthians 7:2-4.

Reckon: Romans 6:11; Galatians 2:20.

Resist: Matthew 4:10; James 4:7-8.

Restoration: Psalm 51:10; Luke 22:31-32.

Secret Sins: Numbers 32:23; Psalm 90:7-8; Matthew 10:26.

Spiritual War: 1 Peter 2:11; Revelation 12:17.

Standards: Isaiah 32:8; Ephesians 5:3; 1 Peter 1:15-16.

Temptation: Luke 4:13; 1 Corinthians 10:13; James 1:13-15.

The Body: Romans 6:12-13; 1 Corinthians 6:18-20.

The Conscience: Acts 24:16; 1 Timothy 1:5.

The Eyes: Job 31:1; Psalm 101:2-3; Proverbs 27:20.

The Heart: Matthew 15:18-19; Psalms 119:9, 11.

The Holy Spirit: John 14:26; Romans 8:12-13; Galatians 5:22-23;
          Ephesians 5:18.

Thoughts: Romans 8:5-7; 2 Corinthians 10:3-5;
          Philippians 4:8; Colossians 3:1-2.

Weapons: Ephesians 6:17; 2 Peter 1:3-4.

ROBERT DANIELS is available to speak to men's groups on the battle for sexual purity. The publisher will forward all requests and correspondence to the author.

APPENDIX

The following is what I call a "Purity Pack" of Scripture verses—several verses for each topic. I suggest that you memorize the topic as well as the verses, and the reference too. Ask God to give you a partner to memorize these verses with. That way you can have someone to encourage you, and you can encourage him. I repeat each verse twenty-five times out loud and learn it well enough to say it word perfect before moving onto another verse.

As you memorize these verses, you will find Psalm 119:9, 11 becoming a reality—"How can a young man keep his way pure? By living according to your word. . . . I have hidden your word in my heart that I might not sin against you."

Accountability: Hebrews 10:24-25; James 5:16

Attitude: Romans 13:13-14; Colossians 3:5-7.

Consequences: Proverbs 5:7-14; 1 Corinthians 6:9-11; Hebrews 13:4.

Destiny of the Pure: Matthew 5:8; Ephesians 1:4; Colossians 1:22.

Discipline: Proverbs 5:21-23; 2 Timothy 2:20-22; Hebrews 12:5-7.

Flee: Genesis 39:12; 2 Timothy 2:22.

Forgiveness: Psalm 32; 51; 1 John 1:9.